Warning!

Climbing is an inherently dangerous sport in which severe injuries or death may occur. Relying on the information in this book may increase the danger.

When climbing you can only rely on your skill, training, experience, and conditioning. If you have any doubts as to your ability to safely climb any route in this guide, do not try it.

This book is neither a professional climbing instructor nor a substitute for one. It is not an instructional book. Do not use it as one. It contains information that is nothing more than a compilation of opinions about climbing in Alaska. These opinions are neither facts nor promises. Treat the information as opinions and nothing more. Do not substitute these opinions for your own common sense and experience.

Assumption of Risk

There may be errors in this book resulting from the mistakes of the author and/or the people with whom they consulted. The information was gathered from a variety of sources, which may not have been independently verified. Those who provided the information may have made mistakes in their descriptions. The author may have made mistakes in his conveyance of the information in this book. The author cannot, therefore, guarantee the correctness of any of the information contained in this book. The topographical maps, photo-diagrams, difficulty ratings, protection ratings, approach and/or descent information, suggestions about equipment, and other matters may be incorrect or misleading. Fixed protection may be absent, unreliable, or misplaced. You must keep in mind that the information in this book may be erroneous, so use your own judgement when choosing, approaching, climbing, or descending from a route described in this book.

DO NOT USE THIS BOOK UNLESS YOU [AND YOUR ESTATE] PROMISE NEVER TO TRY TO SUE US IF YOU GET HURT OR KILLED.

Disclaimer of Warranties

THE AUTHOR AND PUBLISHER WARN THAT THIS BOOK CONTAINS ONLY THE AUTHOR'S OPINIONS ON THE SUBJECTS DISCUSSED. WE MAKE NO OTHER WARRANTIES EXPRESSED OR IMPLIED, OF MERCHANTABILITY, FITNESS FOR PURPOSE, OR OTHERWISE, AND IN THE EVENT, OUR LIABILITY FOR BREACH OF ANY WARRANTY OR CONTRACT WITH RESPECT TO THE CONTENT OF THIS BOOK IS LIMITED TO THE PURCHASE PRICE OF THE BOOK. WE FURTHER LIMIT TO SUCH PURCHASE PRICE OUR LIABILITY ON ACCOUNT OF ANY KIND OF NEGLIGENT BEHAVIOR WHATSOEVER ON OUR PART WITH RESPECT TO THE CONTENTS OF THIS BOOK.

Dghelaya
A Hatcher Pass Climbing Guide

First Edition

by

Kelsey Gray

ISBN: 978-1-7327355-3-8

First Printing April, 2021

Book design: Kelsey Gray, Reinventing the Nomad Publishing
Cover Artwork: Sarah Glaser (sarahkglaser.be)
Cover Design: Amy Strohmeyer
This book was typeset in 9pt Univers
Printed through **Alaska Print Brokers**, Anchorage, Alaska. Printed in China

Published by
Reinventing the Nomad

Anchorage, Alaska
Tel. 907.764.5499
azimuthphoto@gmail.com
This book is available online:

www.climbak.com

APPROACH TIMES

More detailed information on the listed page.

- 0-20 min
- 50-75 min
- 25-45 min
- 80+ min

TABLE OF CONTENTS

REED VALLEY

INDEPENDENCE MINE

PEOPLE

About the Author

Kelsey began climbing in the early 2000s, his first route was Fist Sucker on Sunshine Ridge, and one could say he has been suckered in ever since! Since that fateful day, Kelsey has gone on to teach for the Alaska Rock Gym, organize crag cleanups in Alaska, volunteer with Yosemite Facelift and Covenant House Alaska, mentor new climbers, replace bolts with help from the ASCA, teach climbing courses at UAA and develop new areas around the state. The first edition of the guide required Kelsey to quit his job. Something that really seems to have stuck.

Adventure is a common theme in the Gray family. Through Kelsey's passion for climbing he has roped the rest of the family into the sport. His mother Kimberley and Aunt Elisa climb regularly and even built their own rock wall. The family has climbed together from the Seward Highway to the rocky European cliffs of Gozo, Malta.

In an effort to give back to the climbing community, Kelsey has been working with the American Safe Climbing Association (ASCA) to replace bad, aging, rusted bolts with high grade stainless steel bolts and hangers. Kelsey has replaced over 400 bolts with help from the ASCA. If you are interested in learning more please contact Kelsey to help coordinate the ongoing effort.

Wherever Kelsey goes, whatever he does, it is bound to be related to climbing, be it converting a Whittier bridge into a traverse, climbing in the Arrigetch Peaks, leading in Zion and Yosemite, long routes in Potrero Chico, exploring the Italian Dolomites, cragging in the Verdon Gorge, balancing on basalt columns in Iceland and Panama, or just relaxing on the Seward Highway it is a sure bet that he can be found climbing.

Now Kelsey is currently splitting his time between Thailand and Alaska. Making the summertime pilgrimage to Alaska to develop and gather information for the next edition of this book. Hopefully you enjoy it as much as he did making it.

In my element, staring at a cliff with notes in hand. I often find myself counting bolts on obscure cliffs around the world, before realizing that it is not really necessary. (Courtesy John Borland / morffed.com)

(Courtesy Tom Evans)

Scott Mignery and Jay Rowe preparing to brave the warning on their way to the Monolith in July '90.

Introduction

Hatcher Pass is easily one of the more beautiful and quality cragging areas around Alaska. Granite peaks in alpine valleys with blue lakes set the scene for hundreds of climbs. There is a distinct lack of wildlife in the area other than marmot, ground squirrel, and pika. Many find this as an advantage because, although bears are present in the area and have been seen in places such as Lower Reed Lake, it is uncommon and not normally a threat. The Hatcher Pass climbing area consists primarily of three areas: Reed Lakes, Archangel Valley, and Independence Mine. There are documented climbs along the Glacier Mint trail and in other areas of Hatcher Pass but they are not currently listed within this guidebook. The Hatcher climbing areas were originally combined with the Alaska Rock Climbing Guide. The amount of new development and the growth of the area was going to require enough pages that its own book just made sense. Additionally, this area often requires long approaches and having to carry a brick around isn't always ideal. So it's getting its own book, although the design won't change much.

Reed Lakes is often considered one of the most popular trails in Alaska and it follows the valley to several beautiful glacial blue lakes. The parking area alone had nearly one hundred cars on a single weekend this last summer. The valley has seen a recent resurgence of new routes and is quickly growing to rival Archangel in quantity. It doesn't get as much traffic on the walls but that will likely change as information about the quality of the routes gets out. Especially with the increase in high quality multipitch lines in areas such as the Fatal Attraction Wall, Snowbird Slab, and The High Dive.

Archangel Valley is often thought of as the classic area of Hatcher Pass. The huts have all burned down (some done by the park service itself) but the climbing is just as good as ever. Numerous new areas have grown the amount of routes significantly and even older established areas such as the Gargoyle, are being developed. With the rebolting efforts over the last decade, many of the old button heads are gone and new stainless steel anchors adorn the cliffs. It's a different kind of climbing than before, but hard to complain about! This area even has the added bonus of having an entrance exam: a road that will threaten your oil pan at every chance. If you have a car that's low to the ground, you might want to consider another area.

Independence Mine grew quickly and now nearly 50 climbs with a great selection of multi pitch and difficult routes can be found. It is always a challenge to develop in this area where the rights of property owners spill into the state park and cliffs can be found to be "off limits" relatively quickly. Ownership of these areas is complicated but it is best to follow the signs or ask other climbers about access. While it can be frustrating to have a climbing area off-limits, it can be even more frustrating to lose another one because of a lack of care by other climbers. Beyond the property rights, it is an incredible valley with easy parking access (although the gate tends to close as early as 7 pm) and trails throughout. Everything is closer than it originally appears and most approaches are easy to follow.

Hatcher Pass is not an area to miss, and despite its previous reputation of being scary, dangerous, or runout, the new Hatcher has a lot more to offer for all levels and abilities. I often hear from climbers who have avoided Hatcher because of its reputation for danger. This idea should change over time as these new routes and replacement efforts have changed the landscape of climbing in Hatcher Pass.

Getting Here

Let's be honest, you're going to fly here or live here if you plan on cragging. If you drive from Seattle to climb at Hatcher Pass, you deserve extra cool points.

Getting to Anchorage:

Fly: Its the best option you have and how most will likely reach Alaska. Since Delta and JetBlue began flights to Alaska it has lowered the price of most tickets with some being around $99 for a RT to Seattle. It doesn't get much better than that.

Drive: It is also possible to drive to Anchorage, from Seattle this takes about 40 non-stop hours and 2400 miles. It's an incredible drive and well worth it in its own right, but obviously not for just a crag.

From Anchorage to Hatcher Pass (South)

Access into the valley is restricted to one road. Those coming from Anchorage will use the East approach, which is the most common. The fastest way to approach Hatcher Pass is to take Trunk Rd. From the Glenn Hwy stay on the highway as it goes left to Wasilla. Take the Trunk Road exit and follow Trunk Road for 6 miles until it runs into Palmer-Fishook Road Turn left and it will lead into Hatcher Pass.

Steve Garvey preparing for a day of climbing in the late 80's. (Courtesy Larry Nelson)

2nd Option: After entering Palmer take the Glenn Hwy to leave town toward Glennallen. After just a few short miles there will be a large sign on the right signaling a left turn for Independence Mine State Historical Park. Take a left onto Palmer-Fishook Rd and it will turn into Hatcher Pass Rd after a few minutes.

Archangel Valley, Roadhouse Rock, and Reed Valley are all accessed by a dirt road that has taken more than one oil pan from its parent vehicle. The road will take a very sharp left and head uphill continuing as Hatcher Pass Road. After less than a mile there will be a dirt road on the right labeled Archangel Road.

From Willow to Hatcher Pass (West)

Approach from the West is by Willow-Fishhook Road which turns into Hatcher Pass Road somewhere around Twelvemile Lake. This is a windy dirt road that will test if all bolts on your vehicle are tight enough not to rattle loose. Willow-Fishhook Road is Mile 71 on the Parks Highway. This portion of the road is usually closed to car traffic between September - May.

Archangel Road Information

Archangel Road is often closed from the beginning of winter until whenever the park service feels like opening the gate, possibly in late May but usually early June. If the gate is closed it becomes a 3 mile walk or bike to most of the climbing, Roadhouse Rock is first at 1 mile. Driving down the road can be an adventure of its own. Usually the best portion of the road is the first 1.5 miles until a bridge that crosses a swift creek. Immediately after this bridge is the parking area for Reed Lakes. Driving after this point is only recommended for vehicles with high clearance although you will see the occasional Saturn at the end of the road showing it is possible to get there, if not a little damaging. As a courtesy, if you see someone driving the road leaking some type of automotive fluid, it's fine to let them know.

Independence Mine Information

An easier crag to get to by a vehicle with low clearance because you never drive off the pavement. If it is late in the season you can drive to the top visitor parking area. If not, then add another 10-15 minutes for the extra walk. The gate for the mine usually closes at 7pm and they will close you in. You might be able to get them to let you out but it is not always guaranteed.

Independence Mine State
Historical Park Visitor Center
(open seasonally) Parking $5
907.745.2827

Weather

This area could have a book all its own, or it could be contained on one flash card : Expect rain. That being said it really depends on the year. Some years you wonder if it is ever going to stop raining, and eventually you see the odd dedicated individual hiking off in the rain to try their hand at some wet granite cragging. Then a summer comes along that makes us all forget just how bad it can get, beautiful bluebird days and dry rock abound. The normal weather pattern on sunny days is a beautiful morning leads into afternoon showers that fade away in a few hours. On bad days its rains all day, then week, then seemingly forever. You can't trust anything that a weather person says (sorry meteorologist), their track record with Hatcher is notoriously unreliable. You can check the webcam for the Marmot area online but that will only give you a glimpse of one area. These valleys can be significantly different even just across the ridge line. The best bet is to drive out and check it for yourself, you likely won't know what it is like until you're standing at the approach. Here is a rundown of what to expect from month to month.

Oct - April - In some cultures there are special months considered Fall and Spring that fall into this range. In Hatcher this period is referred to as winter. It is entirely possible to climb during some periods of these months but often require long approaches through the snow and wet rock. Boulderers may tell you that these are some great times as the snow doubles for crashpads.

May - The gate to Archangel Valley may open near the end of May, which begins a flood of climbers into the area. The road is usually partially dry and climbers start to make their early pilgrimages. The weather can be fickle with even the occasionally late season snow but sun is not uncommon. Independence Mine area approaches will be primarily snow but are also accessible and some of the crags will be drying out by this point.

June - The goods appear. During a normal year, much of the snow will be gone along the approaches. There will still be patches and it is important to note that deep chasms exist between the boulders. It is not hard to get hurt if you fall into one of these. The Archangel gate opens reducing the approach between 1-3 miles and Independence Mine is open for business, eliminating an extra mile of approach.

July - This is the month you take off from work, or just quit your job. It's easier that way. On good years you'll be able to climb nearly every day and temperatures can reach into the 80's. Hikers fill the parking lots but there is plenty of rock to be had. Climb every day you can. Afternoon rains can still be common and on average years you can expect at least half of the days to be rain free.

August - It's always hard to know what is going to happen in August. It usually rains more and occasionally the snow will start to fall. Temperatures definitely drop, Renaissance Wall turns into an ice box, and you'll see berry pickers everywhere. Expect more rain, daily showers as well as all day pours.

September - There is a final season rush that always happens in September. The snow is threatening to fall, or has begun already, but days of sunshine still persist. Temperatures drop quickly and its important to dress correctly as a sunny day can open up in a rain / snow within the hour. There tend to still be a few good days for sending those late season projects and finishing up before the winter comes.

Geology

Hatcher Pass, located in the Talkeetna Mountains, boasts the best easily accessible granite in Southcentral Alaska and some of the worst weather. Although notorious for rain, a sunny day will remind you why a venture into Hatcher Pass is a gamble worth taking. The rocks are the only granitic rocks in the greater area, and they are well worth climbing. To climbers the granite will feel solid and usually grippy. Those who bolt will find that it is often porous and, depending on the area, a drill bit will last longer in Hatcher than on the Seward Highway. If you're placing gear it can be easy to get comfortable on the granite, especially if you've spent a lot of time in other areas of Southcentral Alaska but it is still important to tap check (hitting the rock with your fist or palm to feel and listen to the hollowness of the rock) before trusting your life to a big fall. While there is plenty of good rock, you'll often find that the cracks can be crumbly with the rock resembling kitty litter. The granite also has a propensity for fracturing or plating, where whole sections come off in slices rather then big chunks. This can have a quick negative effect when the side of a crack comes apart with your gear alongside it.

The geology of Hatcher Pass is quite interesting when viewed on a geologic map. There are actually two different rock units that split the Reed Valley and Archangel Valley climbing areas. Although they are similar, they do have a few differences. The rock that comprises the Reed Lakes area is considered tonalite of early Paleocene and Late Cretaceous age. Radiometric dates from this pluton range from 67 to 73 million years old. It is a large granitic pluton of predominately biotite-hornblende tonalite and lesser biotite-hornblende quartz diorite. This area occupies most of the Little Susitna and Kashwitna Rivers in the western Talkeetna Mountains.

Archangel Valley and the surrounding areas are part of the Willow Creek Pluton, which is Late Cretaceous in age. Radiometric dates from the pluton range from 72 to 79 million years old. It is pervasively altered, zoned pluton occupying much of the headwaters of Willow Creek. As with Reed Valley it is composed of granitic intrusions, mostly quartz diorite. Generally the rocks are medium grained; the main ingredients are plagioclase, quartz, biotite, and hornblende. There are lesser concentrations of magnetite, zircon, microcline, orthoclase, sphene, and apatite. Both of these plutons were formed from a partially liquid magma that pushed and rose upward. It eventually crystallized at least several kilometers below the Earth's surface. Around 15-20 million years ago tectonic activity brought these rocks to the Earth's surface. Glaciers and streams have subsequently scoured the landscape revealing what we see today.

Brock Rust on the underrated climb Unknown 420 at Green Gully. The Green Gully is packed with high quality lines. (Courtesy Jim Schloemer)

Equipment

Having a great day in Hatcher Pass may come entirely down to bringing the proper gear. This list can help you make sure you're prepared to climb.

Trad Gear: Generally a standard rack will get you through many climbs. I consider a standard rack to be one of each size cam from 0.25" to 3". There are some climbs where it helps to have gear to 4", but gear to 5" is more rare. The majority of trad climbs are not perfect cracks like you can find in some of the more popular granite areas like Squamish or Yosemite. They tend to be inconsistent and fractured with a wide range of gear sizes on a single climb. There are also a lot of climbs that are mixed, with even just one piece of gear making the difference between safe and runout. While it may seem strange to leave a bolted route with a single piece of gear, it is the ethic of the area that gear placements should be left unbolted.

Sport Gear: Many of the old rusty anchors were replaced in the last decade, these new anchors will usually have chains or rap rings and some even have hooks for lowering. This means that most climbers won't need to bring extra cord or rap rings to leave at rappel stations. The old anchors still exist, so it may still be good to have some extra cord on you, but they are not as common as they used to be. A set of 15 draws will be fine in Hatcher with as little as 10 getting you through most of the climbs. Bringing several extendable draws (slings) can really help to reduce rope drag and make sure the rope doesn't run over sharp edges.

Steve Garvey bolting Makin' Hole (5.10c) at the Dorsal Fin, on lead. July '92 (Courtesy Tom Evans)

Aleah DeNuptiis wishing she'd brought her comfy shoes. Hatcher is a place where comfortable shoes are ideal. (Courtesy Kate Day)

Brain Buckets: Helmets are a must. Rocks are constantly falling from above and around climbs. Alright, so maybe it isn't constant, but it should be thought of as that way. One life was likely saved in Hatcher this year due to a helmet. Wear a helmet.

Rope: Many climbs will be perfectly fine with a 60m rope, but a 70m rope is better for Hatcher. There are plenty of pitches where rappelling with a 60m won't make it or will be closer than is considered safe. Newer climbs tend to be pushing these limits as 70m ropes become more of a standard than novelty. The height should be listed on all routes that are nearing 30m. Check to make sure your rope will make it down and always tie knots in the end.

Shoes: Your shoes shouldn't hurt. I know this is somehow not common thought but if someone sold you a pair of shoes promising that they should feel like a foot-binding torture device than you should bring them back. It is true that some shoes will stretch giving your foot a chance to fit them nicely, and really difficult routes require tighter shoes, but if you're not crimping a 5.12 while combing your hair you probably don't need them to hurt. Painful shoes can also lead to lasting foot injuries. Longer climbs mean wearing your shoes for an extended amount of time. You don't want to have your feet hurting too much to continue climbing while miles from the car. Buy shoes that are tight like a sock and don't have extra room near the toe or heel. This can be difficult as climbing shoes are highly variable but try on as many pairs as you can, and ask if they will stretch before buying. Generally leather shoes stretch some and synthetics do not.

Extra Gear: The 10 essentials are a list of items that are meant to prepare you for an emergency in the outdoors. I am editing them slightly as a sort of Hatcher list, but that doesn't mean it's going to make you any safer. This is merely a suggestion. They are as follows:

1. Navigation: A phone is great and all but there is a very obvious lack of service in Hatcher Pass for phones. It'll be spotty at best and should not be relied on. Approaches in this area may put you miles from the car and hours away. This could lead to very slow recovery times for any type of accident or danger. Emergency

Ailsa Faust climbing on Chickenhead at the Monolith, being a model climber by wearing her helmet and warm clothes. (Courtesy Matt Faust)

Happy we brought our gear but wishing for better weather. (Courtesy John Borland)

locator services such as SPOT devices may mean the difference between life or death. Several people have died in Hatcher Pass after getting lost in the fog or rain. At the very least, tell others where you are going.

2. Headlamp: You'll probably be out after dark. With long approaches and fun but challenging climbs it's easy to hike the trail back in the evening, even when the sun doesn't set till 11pm. Twisted ankles and boulder chasms are just a few of the dangers you will want to be able to avoid.

3. Sun protection: While not pivotal, the summer sun can be intense. Bring sunscreen or other protection.

4. First aid: Medical tape, bandages, ace bandage for sprains, painkiller, and a splint are good items to carry in Hatcher.

5. Knife: Useful for cutting webbing too, double purpose.

6. Fire: I don't find matches or a lighter that useful in Hatcher Pass. Likely due to the fact that there isn't much to burn.

7. Shelter: Emergency bivy. These can be helpful when the rain hits to shelter against the moisture and wind. Some afternoon storms only last for an hour or two and waiting them out could be your best bet.

8. Extra food: Usually a good idea, you'll burn plenty of calories just getting to the cliff.

9. Extra water: Beyond the minimum. Bring a filter as well, there are usually plenty of places to refill on your way to the crag.

10. Extra clothes: A light rain shell, light poof jacket, and pants are a good list of extras.

Ethics

There are entire college courses devoted to this one word and there could be a degree created just for climbing ethics. Who is to say what you can or cannot do? The true reality is, no one. However, there are certain things which are more accepted than others and if we all adhere to them, then the majority will be content with the climbing scene in Alaska and it can continue to grow. If you plan on developing in a certain area make sure you check the climbs first. See what everyone else has been doing and try talking to those who have already developed there.

Bolting:

Bolting is something that is becoming more common in the climbing world and has been since the 1980's. If done right, it can help create more routes and make some situations much safer. So when is it all right to bolt and when should it be left alone? What type of bolts should be used? Here are a few general rules on bolting, and remember: everyone has a different idea of how, and what, to bolt.

1. Do not bolt a crack. Cracks or other features which offer natural protection should not be bolted. There are some situations where the cracks are of such poor quality that it may necessitate a bolt. Bolted anchors are wonderful and generally accepted when done correctly. However, care should be taken if there is an acceptable place for a natural protection anchor.

2. Using the proper gear. There are many different kinds of bolts and bolt hangers to choose from. These days, it's easy to get stainless steel and it should be used. If you are placing a route near saltwater there are several companies which make marine grade bolts and hangers.

I would like to include much more on this; however, the ethics of bolting in Alaska are still in growth. Areas such as Hatcher Pass have a different attitude than Wiener Lake or Purinton Creek where bolts are plentiful. As the climbing scene evolves, so will the ideas and ethics for each situation.

Bolted Protection:

There are plenty of different types of bolts. Many of the older non-stainless bolts have rusted and are not secure. Originally, the hangers used were SMC, homemade, and Leper hangers with buttonhead bolts. These are no longer secure and should be replaced. It is good to know what a good bolt looks like and what a bad one looks like. Generally if it's rusted and brown, it's an older bolt and should at least be considered suspect. Plenty of bolts have rusted behind the hanger out of view from the climber and the break is often from inside the bolt hole where you can't check it's quality. Recently a lot of rebolting has occurred on many routes along the Seward Highway and Hatcher Pass. Many of these bolts are stamped ASCA and were supplied by the American Safe Climbing Association.

Installing the anchor on top of Cantankerous Cranksters. (Courtesy John Borland)

How to Use This Guide

Every climbing guide has its quirks and I have no doubt that this one is the same. I will try and best describe how to use this guide but some of it just might come down to guesswork. I included descriptions as I felt they would be most easily understood. That means that I will probably be the only one to know where any routes are. I hope to update this book with easier descriptions and information as it becomes available or necessary.

Reading the Route Descriptions:

Each route should be set up similarly. Below is an explanation on how to read the routes. If the route is missing something, then I probably did not have that information.

Route example...

Number — *Route Name* — *Difficulty Rating* — *Star Rating*

1 **Funky Mandibles 5.9** ☆☆☆ **30m** — *Route Height*

Bolts, Gear, and Anchor — 6 bolts, Gear to 2", 2 bolt anchor

Route Description — Bring cams for the lower section to the first bolt or runout on some easy 5.7 climbing. Climb the obvious corner on decent rock.

FA: Kelsey Gray, Aleat Däkling — *First Ascent History*

Number:

Each route description will start with a number. It should be the same as the corresponding number in the overhead topos and pictures. There are two different colors for the numbers. There are many climbs with multiple pitches. I included all of the pitches when I list it sport or trad. It is possible for the first pitch of a climb to be all sport and the second pitch to use gear. Read the gear descriptions for extra information.

1 Red indicates a sport route, which means it can be done without traditional gear and usually on quickdraws. Some routes may require a few pieces of gear to help eliminate runouts but it will be labeled a sport route if it is sufficient without traditional protection. Red is also used to indicate toprope routes.

2 Blue indicates a route that is climbed with traditional protection. It does not mean that there are no bolts, it only means that the route is done more safely with gear.

Route Name:

The name will come immediately after the identifying route number. Not all routes will have names. Some areas were much more difficult to gather information on and I have ended up with several unknowns. Remember, just because it has *Unknown* for a name doesn't mean it is a bad route!

Difficulty Rating:

The ratings in the book are based on the Yosemite Decimal System. When I began this book, many of the routes in areas such as Hatcher Pass did not have the now standard letter grading system. Most would say "5.10+" instead of "5.10d". I tried to update many of the ratings to include letter grades. I determined the difficulty by climbing the route and combining that with the comments from other climbers. Everyone will feel different when climbing and something which felt hard to me may not feel as difficult to others. If you don't feel that I have graded a route correctly then please send me a message and let me know what you think. A few rare climbs may have a climbing grade and then a question mark at the end. This means that it is either an unfinished project or I had no information from which to get the grade. Hopefully these will be added soon. In the case of multi-pitch routes, I tried to include a rating for each pitch. There is a free climbing grade conversion chart that can be found on page 12.

PG13 = Not quite as runout as an "r" rating but there is some distance between bolts.
r = Runout between placements or bolts.
x = A fall means probable injury or death. This could also indicate a route that has no anchor or finish.

Star Rating

Not all routes are made the same. Some are high quality and some should never be attempted again. I use a star rating for a majority of the climbs. Throughout my travels I found it nice to open a local guidebook and see climbs rated by the author and others who have climbed them, so I decided to do the same. I am using a 5 star system with 5 stars being great and one star being terrible. If it doesn't have a star rating it still may be a quality route, it just means I may not have known what rating to apply. There is also a bomb that is used throughout the book and especially along the Seward Highway to indicate routes that are beyond bad but are generally considered very dangerous. The single star was misleading people into believing the climb may be "not so bad". Hopefully, a bomb is more clear that the climb should be avoided.

💣 - Not worth the trouble, dirty, or dangerous.
☆ - It's not necessarily dangerous but it ain't good either.
☆☆ - Not so great, lackluster, worth it if you are bored, maybe.
☆☆☆ - Good route, decent quality and generally enjoyable.
☆☆☆☆ - Great route, worth going to the crag for.
☆☆☆☆☆- Classic, call in to work because you're not going in today.

One more thing to keep in mind: not all crags are the same. A 5 star climb on the Seward Highway may only be a 3 star in Hatcher Pass. The climbs are graded by area, a good thing to remember when you are about to get on a 2 star Seward Highway climb.

Bolts, Gear, and Anchor

I tried to get all the information necessary for gear and bolts on the climbs. Although I made the effort to be exact on the bolt count, I would recommend you always bring a few extra quickdraws and plan ahead. I like to say, "Whatever the guidebook says, plus two." Alaska has many old manky bolts which need to be replaced and most are located in Hatcher Pass. When climbing on these bolts always be aware that they are many years old, need replacing, and shouldn't be fallen on. Some of the older bolts in Hatcher Pass have come out by body weight alone. Don't let that discourage you from visiting the area, as many bolts were replaced in the last eight years. I also tried to separate pins and bolts. If there is gear such as pitons, knifeblades, RURP's (Realized Ultimate Reality Piton), pins, and others, I listed them simply as "pitons". Know what you are getting into when you clip one.

To make it easier to understand, I use common terminology for gear throughout the book. When I put a gear suggestion, that is

Cristian Ortega and Fernando Martinez Batiz reading up on the next pitch on Sunshine Ridge (p.64). (Courtesy John Peacock)

exactly what it is, a suggestion. Not everyone will use the same pieces of gear so remember to come prepared. There is a glossary of terms in the back of the book if any of the gear names I use are confusing. In the guide I use the term, "TCU"; this means tri-camming unit. When I say trad rack, that means bring an assortment of all sizes of gear, usually up to 3".

Anchors are often in the same condition as the regular bolts. Some anchors are so old they should not be used until replaced. Between 2011 and 2020 many bolts and anchors have been replaced thanks in large part to the ASCA supplying hardware. In the book I try to make a note if the anchors are bad, hopefully they will be replaced over time. There are many different types of anchors and I tried to list what each was. Here is a list of the anchor types included in this book:

Bolt anchor - I have tried to count the bolts for each anchor in this book. Just because it says there is a bolt anchor does not mean that it is a solid one. Some need replacing. There are times when it will say, "1 bolt + 1 chain anchor". This means that one of the bolts does not have a regular hanger, instead it has a small piece of chain attached directly to the bolt.

Typical new anchor setup with two types of quicklinks or rings to help lower rope twist. (Courtesy Eric Roberts)

Rap anchor - New to this guidebook is this category of anchor. The rebolting effort has created many anchors with large rap rings or other rappel setup. These anchors are ready for rappel and should not require any hardware of your own to rappel from. Please don't leave any equipment at the anchor, such as webbing, if you see these nice new anchors with rings or quicklinks on them. Many anchors are setup for rappel but may not say "rap anchor" since this category is new it will take time to change the anchor type in the book.

Chain anchor - All chain anchors will be on bolts. Chain is usually a large piece of stainless or non-stainless chain which is attached for easy belaying and lowering. Remember never run your rope directly through a normal hanger unless they are rap hangers made for the purpose. Chain often allows you to run your rope directly through for rappelling. Do not toprope through the chain; always use a carabiner. This category will be phased out and replaced by "rap anchor".

Sling anchor - This means that, at the time, there was webbing or pieces of rope being used as an anchor. If it does not say anything about bolts such as, "2 bolt sling anchor", then the webbing is used to sling boulders or vegetation.

Gear anchor - Usually this means there is a crack nearby where you can use natural protection to create an anchor. Remember to bring an assortment of gear for the anchor, including long slings.

Steve Garvey's slung horn and gear anchor up near The Guardian. (Courtesy Larry Nelson)

No anchor - The most obvious, there is no anchor found nor a decent place to use a gear anchor. Usually this means there is a walk-off and a hip belay is in order.

Tree anchor - There are climbs that only have trees for the anchor. The best thing to remember about trees is that every time we use them to anchor we weaken the tree. There are several bolted anchors now where trees have fallen, partially due to climbers.

A night climber at Goats Head Soup. (Courtesy Regan Marin)

Recently, thanks to the American Safe Climbing Association, many bolts were replaced along the Seward Highway and in Hatcher Pass. You can find a list of some of these routes on the ASCA's website (*http://www.safeclimbing.org/*). Hopefully with their continued assistance Alaska's old bolts will be new once again.

Route Description:

Each route should have a description. I tried to include some general geographical points to help find the route. It can be quite hard to describe where a route is, so I included pictures and overhead topographical maps to help. You may find things such as, "starts on a right leaning ramp" and it will seem that every route starts on a right leaning ramp. Hopefully through the growing of this guide, route descriptions will become clearer. This will also be where route variations can be found and will usually take the format of "Var.1: 5.9" or similar. If it is a multipitch climb then the pitches will be broken up by information throughout the description starting with the pitch number and including the rating, gear, and anchor. Any other important route information will be found in this section.

ALL ROUTE MEASUREMENTS MAY BE WRONG! Now that I have your attention I want to tell you about route measurements. Try looking at an object outside your window and take a guess at how far away it is. That's what we do for many route measurements. These are merely suggestions and you should always tie knots in the end of your rope when lowering a climber or rappelling, or assume you may not make it. All measurements in this book for route lengths are done in meters. Most ropes are 50m or 60m. The route measurements are from ground to anchor and are usually estimates. So if it says 32m after the route description make sure to bring at least a 70m rope or two 60's for the rappel because 64m of rope will be necessary for a single rope rappel. Many of these estimates are entirely on our best guess. Do not assume they are perfect and always pay attention to the end of your rope.

ALWAYS TIE KNOTS IN THE END OF YOUR ROPE WHEN RAPPELLING OR LOWERING!

First Ascent History:

At the bottom of most route descriptions is a section that says "FA:", this is used to indicate first ascent. Many routes still have Unknown listed and it will take everyone's help to fill in these holes. If the area for FA is left blank, it is unknown or may still be waiting for the first ascent.

FA = First Ascent

FFA = First Free Ascent

Other Images and Meanings:

There are other images, color schemes, and oddities located throughout this guide. Below is a list of their meanings:

- Sunlight. No AM or PM = Sun all day
- Approach time to crag or area
- Obvious tree
- Overhanging wall or mountainside
- Normal Vertical Wall
- Vegetated ramp, gully, or flat land
- Trails
- Denotes a bolted anchor in a multipitch climb
- Denotes a gear anchor in a multipitch climb

Reflections of Hatcher Pass

by Kathy Rowe

It was a sunny July evening in 1986 when Jay Rowe and I bumped along the primitive Archangel Road and pulled into the Webfoot parking lot. We had recently driven from Washington in a borrowed 1968 VW Bug to spend the summer together. I was born and raised in Alaska and was eager to show my future husband the magic of Hatcher Pass.

Jay Rowe climbing up to Roger's Roof at the Upper Lane Walls. (Courtesy Kathy Rowe)

After donning our packs we eagerly scanned the nearby climbing possibilities. The rock across the river looked promising and we headed that direction. As we walked past the miner's cabin we came across two ruggedly handsome, spicy young men lounging by a fire after a day of climbing. We all introduced ourselves and had a cordial visit. After crossing the river the Cheechako Block Wall caught Jay's eye. There was no guide book, but later we found out that he attempted a climb called Right Trident Crack. As he worked his way up the climb, we could hear shouts coming from the cabin across the river, perhaps from our new friends. We weren't sure if it was cheering or heckling. Later we chatted with them and learned that they had been working the same climb earlier that day and Jay had apparently challenged their high point. Conclusion… heckling! Jay didn't get up the entire route, but he got far enough to get their attention.

Little did we know this would be the start of lasting friendships with Steve Garvey and Jim Sweeney, who just happened to be two of the area's most prolific climbers. Soon to follow would be Jay's apprenticeship with Steve, and it wasn't long before they were calling each other at 4:00am to be on the ice by first light. Steve's strong opinions lead to many a spirited conversation about climbing, modifying gear, relationships and kids. Eventually Steve married Lynne, the love of his life, and our friendship with the two of them deepened. Jay also enjoyed a fun partnership with Jim. They climbed together many times, and eventually made early attempts on both Broken Tooth and Sugar Tooth in the Alaska Range.

For many years we would make numerous trips to the Lane

Kathy, Jay, Carson, and Kayla Rowe enjoy camping at the Lane Prospect. (Courtesy Kathy Rowe)

Kathy Rowe on Checkered Dog (5.9) on the Monolith sporting her favorite shoes, LaSportiva Mega's, in 1989. (Courtesy Jay Rowe)

Prospect. During the endless warm summer days, we explored the wonders of the area and returned each night to the well-stocked Lane Hut to sleep. After climbing, my love of photography found me stalking small mammals while Jay napped in the tundra, lulled to sleep by the sound of babbling brooks. Evenings would find Jay taping pictures into a notebook and writing route descriptions next to them to leave for others. It was a carefree and magical time.

Some years later when we had our son, Carson, and daughter, Kayla, Steve gave us a lecture about how to make the mountains fun for kids. He said with fervent conviction, "You've got to bring LOTS of stuffed animals, pillows and chocolate!" Thanks to Steve, our children enjoyed many indulgent treats on our outdoor adventures.

We raised our kids with frequent visits to Hatcher Pass, floating rubber ducks down streams, playing "Marmot" amongst the boulders, exploring mine shafts, and eventually putting them on rope. At first it seemed they would rather frolic in the tundra than climb a rock. Then, slowly as they grew, it was fun to see them develop their climbing skills.

Presently, both kids are grown and leading busy, productive lives. However, it seems that the time we spent at Hatcher must have made a lasting impression because whenever they come home to visit, our family makes a beeline for a new adventure there. It was a proud moment in 2018 when Jay was able to climb Toto with Kayla and her husband, Miles Knotek. The area continues to serve as an idyllic, unforgettable place to experience the mountains. It feels good to know our love for Hatcher has been passed on to the next generation. Wherever our kids land, I hope they will discover more adventures and lasting memories creating their version of Hatcher Pass.

Kathy Rowe in an ore cart at the Entrance to Crystal Caves Shaft in Hatcher Pass. (Courtesy Kathy Rowe)

Hatcher Pass

Jay Swartly leading Tunnel Vision (5.11d) with Sagar Gondalia on belay. The haze is from the heavy smoke from the seasonal wildfires. (Courtesy Sarah Conlin)

Tsaltastnu Tl'u is the name of the Little Susitna River area near Independence Mine. It means "River Headwaters" to the Upper Cook Inlet Dena'ina.

44 Areas
375 Routes
Difficulties from 5.4 to 5.13d
80 Miles from Anchorage
Season : April - September

Why Dghelaya?

Dghelaya translates to "mountain," in the language of the Upper Cook Inlet Dena'ina. This word can be seen in multiple names of features in the area such as Tsałtastnu Dghelaya (Montana Peak). This name was chosen for the guidebook through several conversations with indigenous members, in an effort to promote the cultural significance of the language without appropriating for profit.

I've always wondered why the only history that we seem to have for Hatcher Pass is based entirely on miners. In fact, you can still see their leftover remnants. These garbage items are considered history, and for some reason that means they can leave them rotting in the rivers. But what about those who came before the miners? Where has their history gone?

This is the question that led me to learn more about the Upper Cook Inlet Dena'ina. The Upper Cook Inlet area has been inhabited for at least 10,000 years. The most recent tribe who called this land home, prior to the miners and colonists, are known as the Dena'ina. They have inhabited this area for over a thousand years and have a rich language with many names for the surrounding geography. These words can often be hard to pronounce and that has led to the renaming of basically everything. But this isn't a culture that died off before the Russians sold the land to the United States of America. The Dena'ina still exist, carrying their history forward.

Recently, there has been a movement in Alaska toward returning the names of geographic features to the original names used by the local indigenous peoples. The town of Barrow was returned to Utqiagvik, and in the most famous example, Mt. Mckinley has returned to Denali. As with many indigenous cultures, the rechristening of these features to an English surname or word not only removes a historical name, but erases the language. Many of the indigenous words have meaning and often describe an event or area. The name for Government Peak in Hatcher Pass is K'eda Beq'e Nay'uni, which translates to "The One That Has a Horn on It." Renaming the peak may not only lose that name but the historical importance of that area and all the words associated with it. Hopefully, you will take this information and choose to learn more about the indigenous culture of the Upper Cook Inlet area, as well as wherever your own home may be.

Upper Reed Valley (p.156)
Upper Lane Walls (p.102)
Lower Reed Lake
Didilakama Peak
Lower Reed Valley (p.112)
Lower Lane Walls (p.92)
Fairangel Valley Walls (p.72)
Independence Mine Area (p.164)
The Pinnacle
Lower Webfoot Prospect (p.31)
Reed Lakes Trailhead
Upper Webfoot Prospect (p.56)
Archangel Road Crags (p.19)
Independence Mine
Archangel Road
Gold Mint Trailhead
Palmer-Fishhook Road

These two areas are located along Archangel Road separate from any of the other crags. They are not necessarily close together, but are hard to include in other subareas as they are isolated. Roadhouse Rock is the first crag you come to on Archangel Road and is 1 mile after the turnoff. The Gargoyle comes a lot later, as it is near the end of Archangel Road. The best approach information is located in each section. These crags offer some great and unique climbing and should not be missed.

ARCHANGEL ROAD CRAGS

	CRAG	SUN & HIKE	ROUTES	RANGE	PAGE
1	Roadhouse Rock	30min	20	5.7-5.12b	20
2	The Gargoyle	PM 45min	11	5.7-5.13d	26

Roadhouse Rock 30min

Approach:
Take the turn to Archangel Road and drive 1 mile to the pullout on the right. Park here and Roadhouse Rock is on the left side of the road up the hillside. It looks like a long slog but don't worry, it's been improved. Currently this crag is best climbed in early spring when the vegetation is covered or flat and the approach is much easier. There is a trail that leads to the boulder, but it can be hard to find. From the main parking area for Roadside Crag, walk up the road toward Archangel Valley. Keep an eye out to your left and head up the first section that resembles a trail and leads through the grass, avoiding most of the alders. From Jurassic Park Boulder, trails have been cut in the past but they tend to regrow quickly. It is now a relatively easy hike to get to Jurassic Park and Alpha Wall but can be more of a jungle bushwhack to get to Beta Wall.

Area:
Some of the routes on these walls have a checkered past with routes being described as stolen, contrived, or generally unknown. There is room for more development as there has not been any for over 10 years.

This wall has a beautiful view looking down the valley toward Palmer and into the Mint Peaks. Often late during the day the clouds open up and allow some sun to shine on this area when it is still raining higher up Archangel Road. There is a peaceful feeling to the crag since it is covered in vegetation which, for the most part, stops just at the top of the crag before becoming tundra. Most of the rock in this area resembles the Chugach Front Range more than the rest of Hatcher Pass.

Jurassic Park Boulder 10min

This boulder is located before the main walls on the trail. It is a giant boulder and so some may wonder why there are toprope climbs on it. Really, if you are feeling good about the climb, it's just a highball boulder where a fall could lead to injury. There are bolts on the top for toproping and some difficult climbs. Very few climbs could be done on trad gear and if it were bolted for lead climbing it would only be a bolt or two per route. There are a few climbs worth doing on this little piece of rock, even though they take imagination.

1 Steggy 5.7 ☆☆ **6m**
Toprope, 2 bolt rap anchor
Easy big ledges on the left side of the boulder. It is the easiest line on the face and will finish just right of the upper alder.

2 Where Are The Kids? 5.11c ☆☆☆ **6m**
Toprope, 2 bolt rap anchor
Climb direct on the face between two black streaks using awkward and crimpy holds and fun movements.

3 Cave Dweller 5.12b ☆☆ **7m**
Toprope, 2 bolt rap anchor
Start in the cave and move left to a corner for real trickery or start on the boulders for an easier beginning. Climb into the corner staying left of the arete to a mossy ledge. Protect your shoulders.

4 Down the Spine 5.12a ☆☆☆☆ **7m**
Toprope, 2 bolt rap anchor
Start in the small cave and climb the arete direct to a ledge. Fun, tricky moves will get you up the arete.

5 Jurassic Park 5.11a ☆☆☆ **7m**
Toprope, 2 bolt rap anchor
Begin on a thin corner crack above a ledge which is waist high. Move right with the corner then pull onto a larger ledge. Climb onto a grassy ramp to the anchors. May be possible to climb on small gear.
FA: Steve Garvey

6 Clever Girl 5.12a ☆☆ **8m**
Toprope, 2 bolt rap anchor
Climb up the orange and black slab with crimps. Climb direct to keep the hard rating; moving right or left too far will make this climb easier.

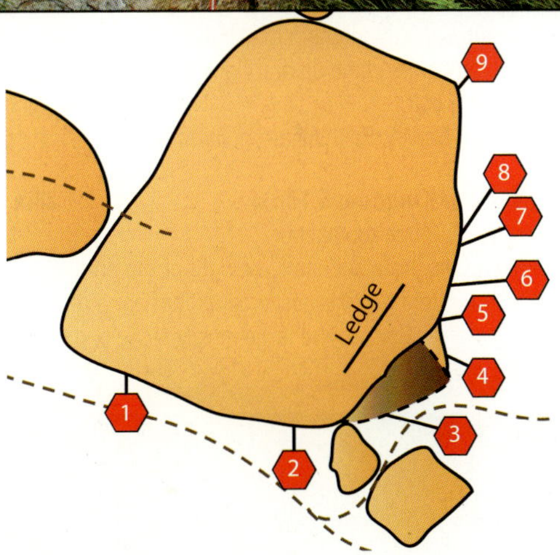

7 Spared No Expense 5.9+ ☆☆ **8m**
Toprope, 1 bolt, 2 bolt rap anchor
1 meter right of *Clever Girl*. Climb the orange slab moving right to easier holds but stay off the right leaning ramp. There is one bolt above the climb for a directional.

8 Awkward Sequels 5.8 ☆☆☆ **8m**
Toprope, 1 bolt, 2 bolt rap anchor
Climb the right angling ledges which end near the right corner of the rock. This could be climbed on small gear but probably wouldn't be a very enjoyable lead. There is a bolt above and left of the climb for a directional.

9 Hands of Engineers 5.10a ☆☆ **8m**
Toprope, 1 bolt, 2 bolt rap anchor
Start around the corner near a boulder and traverse right along the arete to the face. Climb direct to the top and 1 bolt on the ramp, continue on the ramp to the anchor.

Alpha Wall 20min

Walking through the alders further up the hill from the Jurassic Park Boulder will bring you to a short cliff section. The rock in this area tends to be lower quality on the bottom half of the cliff but fun and relatively good on the upper half. This area resembles the Chugach Front Range in rock type and quality. Climb with care and be careful of the eagles which have been known to nest on the large grass ledge in the middle of the cliff. If you do see birds nesting, please do not climb on this section of the cliff and leave the birds alone. To get to this area walk up left of the Jurassic Park Boulder toward a triangular shaped cliff. The trail to the wall can be good one year and gone the next. The best way to get to the crag is to plan ahead and look for grassy areas that avoid the alders.

1 Unknown 5.10d/r ☆☆☆ 28m

5 bolts, Gear to 2", 2 bolt rap anchor

Start in an obvious corner with a bolt 3 meters up. Use enjoyable stemming through this section which has some loose blocks. Climb to a large vegetated ledge and continue into another small bolted corner. Once out of the corner climb up and right meeting with *Mugs Route* at a bolt.

FA: Steve Garvey, Paul Wharton, Jim Sweeney

2 Moss Kingdom 5.10c 28m

Gear to 1", 2 bolt rap anchor

Begin on the arete and stay just right of the arete. Bring a nut tool to clean placements that are already slim pickings. Goes to the large mossy ledge and one bolt.

3 Mugs Route 5.10c/r ☆☆ 28m

2 bolts, Gear to 2", 2 bolt rap anchor

Start in a mossy and dirty dihedral. This is about as much fun as setting your toe hairs on fire. Once out of the dihedral, pull on moss and grass to gain the large ledge with one bolt. I would recommend toproping from this bolt and climbing *Unknown #1* first if you really feel the need to climb it. There are plenty of loose holds on this section. The portion after the large ledge is actually enjoyable and worth a trip up. Continue through cracks and a few bolts. Move left to the same anchor as the previous climb. This climb was done shortly after the death of Mugs Stump.

FA: Jim Sweeney, Steve Garvey, Paul Wharton

Beta Wall 35min

In this area I included all the upper portions of the cliff. The rock for most of these climbs is higher quality than the Alpha Wall and it has been compared with Eldorado Canyon in Colorado. It is worth the effort to get to some of these climbs so you should take the time to go if you have never been to this area.It gets nice late afternoon light and has a great view over the valley. This is also the area with the most development at Roadhouse Rock.

1 Garvey Arete 5.9 ☆☆ **12m**

3 bolts, 2 bolt rap anchor

The only climb on this small portion of wall moves just left of the arete over awkward moves with a slight runout spacing of the bolts. The anchor was replaced in 2017.

FA: Steve Garvey

2 Blueberries 5.8 ☆ **21m**

Gear to 3", No anchor

Climbs the dihedral on the left. Bad pro at the start that improves slightly on the way up. Make note that there is no anchor at the top and this route has received a good deal of vegetation over the years.

FA: Jim Sweeney, Mike Tumey 09.09.1988

3 Ramblin' Rover 5.10b/r ☆☆☆ **20m**

4 bolts, 1 piton, Gear to .75", 2 bolt rap anchor

First bolt is 5 meters off the deck. Climb up left and move to the bolt, don't deck. Continue over bulges through the climb. Rock is muggy even when dry so bring your chalk. Move up right after the last bolt to the anchor. A walkoff is possible but less enjoyable.

FA: Roger Pollard, Grant Walker

4 It Takes a Thief 5.11c ☆☆☆½ **18m**

7 bolts, 2 bolt anchor

Start low on the cliff, climb high to the first bolt. Move left until the 6th bolt then make a sharp right traverse to the anchors. A hard climb with a middle crux.

FA: Roger Pollard, Grant Walker, Mike Lawson

5 Sourdough Express 5.10b/r ☆☆ 18m
2 bolts, 1 piton, Gear to .5", Alders anchor
Begin on the left side of the dihedral and climb black rock to the roof. Move right to the 2nd bolt and continue through the corner to the topout. A walkoff is possible but annoying. Use slings around alders to anchor, remember that in early season alders may be smaller.
FA: Jim Sweeney, Dave Nyman 09.18.1988

6 Closing Time 5.10a ☆☆☆ 18m
1 bolt, 2 pitons, Gear to .5", Alders anchor
There are currently two pins on this route and one is a knifeblade. I could go on all day talking about runouts but in Hatcher Pass the game changes a bit. Start just above a collapsed section of the rock and climb to a nice ledge. Continue direct until at the first bolt. Move left or stay on the right face to the finish. Could use an anchor.
FA: Jim Sweeney, Dave Nyman 09.18.1988

7 Cake Walk 5.7 ☆☆☆ 8m
Gear to 3", 2 bolt anchor
Scramble up easy V0 moves to an alder ledge. Continue a few meters up the ledge and you will stumble on a decent hand crack. It's short and ends right when it starts to get fun; an enjoyable climb in its own right. Battle the alders for the anchor.
FA: Jim Sweeney, Dave Nyman

8 The Cave 5.11b ☆☆☆ 15m
Toprope, 2 bolt anchor
In the lower cave there are 2 bolts on the top but no obvious lines that have been completed from what I could see. There is potential for more than this one route if someone wants to bring a drill, not much for pro exists on this wall. Start in the cave and dyno off the jug moving directly into a short corner. Continue up the face. Stays consistently difficult.

(Below) Most of the climbing areas in Hatcher Pass have a great view of the surrounding peaks and routes. Roadhouse Rock is an exception as it is so far down the valley that it comes before most of the rock. This picture shows the way back to Archangel Road. Gold Mint Trail can be seen in the lowest section of the valley. The Gold Mint area is not in this book but the area should not be discounted for the adventurous. There is a lot of great granite and some excellent routes for the strong and willing.

Patrick Harris on the crux of The Romainian Highstep at The Gargoyle.

The Gargoyle PM 45min

Approach:
Getting to the Gargoyle can be an adventure in itself. There is no defined trail and boulder hopping is mandatory. I will only list the easiest approach which I have found for the cliff. When standing at the American Alpine Club's (AAC) outhouse near the end of Archangel Road, locate the cliff high on the mountainside, opposite the Webfoot Prospect climbing areas. The boulder field flows down to the lower portion of the mountain. Look for the flattest section of tundra to cross and make your way direct to the lower boulder field. Once on the field you can cross to the far right where a band of grass comes down or make your way along the boulders. Head direct for the ridge line and the Gargoyle will be watching.

Area:
A recent renaissance in development at the Gargoyle has made it a worthy destination for any climbers willing to test themselves. It has the greatest concentration of hard climbs in the valley, and although the approach is intimidating, it is surprisingly accessible. The hardest climbs on the cliff are sport so you don't even need your rack if you plan to throw yourself at a 5.13. It's an incredible area at the end of the day, receiving the last light to hit Archangel Valley. During the summer you can be climbing at 10pm and still be in the sunlight. It is worth a trip, even if you are just hiking around and want to see a unique area. Be wary of the boulder field as there are some large caves.

This beautiful area has an interesting past. When gathering information for this crag I had two different people tell me they discovered and helped develop the area, although they didn't do it together. The Gargoyle has some odd features which make it different than the other climbing areas in Hatcher Pass. A large tunnel-like passage between the rock and a giant overhanging outcropping give the area several different names, including Pride Rock.

The most defining feature of The Gargoyle is the Pride Rock like formation that juts out over the mountainside. We've all stared at it at some point or another and wondered if the route could go. Now, we may find out.

1 The Alternate 5.12+ ☆☆☆ **7m**
3 bolts, 2 bolt rap anchor
Located on the large overhanging feature. This short route starts on the overhang and heads straight for the lip. It's harder than it looks.
FA: Todd Helgeson 2018

2 Project 5.14
Bolts, 2 bolt rap anchor
This current project follows the bolts along the overhang to end somewhere near the upper end of the feature. It is still in development as of the writing of this book.

3 Goliath Chronicles 5.12a ☆☆☆☆ **15m**
1 bolts, Gear to .75", 2 bolt rap anchor
Start down low and move through excellent climbing in the corner with very small gear, micro stoppers may be helpful. After a rest the crux move awaits at the finish where there is a bolt to protect the move. Lunge your way to success. A great new route and addition to the crag.

4 Unknown 5.11a ☆☆☆ **15m**
6 bolts, 2 bolt rap anchor
Climbs on the arete before the hallway. Climb direct on 6 bolts to the large wedged rock. Run it out at the end or try and find a place for a large cam to pull through the roof crack to the anchors. Can be a scary finishing move.
FA: Paul Turecki, Bob Kahut

5 Crytic Hacker 5.13d ☆☆☆☆ **17m**
6 bolts, 2 bolt rap anchor
Climb the steep face with punchy moves right away. Very little rests on this hard climb that has an incredible view of the valley. The crux is on very insecure and cryptic holds.
FA: Todd Helgeson 2019

6 Inside Chimney 5.8 ☆☆ **13m**
Gear to 3", Slings anchor
Start in the back corner of the hallway and chimney over a large block. Find a good hole to squeeze through for the topout and sling a large boulder at the top. Can often remain wet after a rainfall since it does not get adequate sun to dry quickly inside the chimney. Blocks have moved near the top and continue to do so, the exit may be blocked. Retreat if anything moves.

3
4
5

7 The Romanian Highstep 5.13a ☆☆☆☆ 18m
6 bolts, 2 bolt rap anchor
One of the new hard series of lines on the crag put up by Todd Helgeson. This line got its first ascent late into a summer evening. Clip the first bolt standing high on top of the boulder. Then climb up the clean face with thin moves.
FA: Todd Helgeson 07.04.2020

8 Applied Gothic Architecture 5.11c ☆☆☆ 17m
1 bolt, Gear to 2", 2 bolt rap anchor
A short face leads to a small lip with a bolt below. This a new bolt that was added with permission from the first ascent party. Follow a crack with chickenhead support as it curves to a small ledge
FA: Dave Whitelaw

9 Unknown 5.12a ☆☆☆ 18m
Gear to .5", 2 bolt rap anchor
This rarely climbed line starts just inside the cave. Stem between the two walls using the thin crack for gear; pull onto the left wall from the stem and finish on top. Same anchor as *Applied Gothic Architecture*.
FA: Paul Turecki, Bob Kohut

10 Quatrafoil 5.9 ☆☆ 15m
Gear to 3", Slings anchor
Start on a very defined hand crack which leads to a large scary looking detached flake. Some loose boulders at the top and some other boulders to sling for an anchor.

11 Dripstone 5.7 ☆☆ 15m
Gear to 2", Slings anchor
Short face with a hand crack to a thinner seam. Move left for the topout and boulders to sling for an anchor. This route is hardly worth climbing up to the Gargoyle but if you are there and bored it is another line.

LOWER WEBFOOT PROSPECT

	CRAG	SUN & HIKE	ROUTES	RANGE	PAGE
1	The Diamond	AM 10min	16	5.5-5.11a	32
2	Toto	AM 10min	1	5.7-5.10b	37
3	Zulu Wall	AM 10min	14	5.6-5.12c	40

LOWER WEBFOOT PROSPECT

	CRAG	SUN & HIKE	ROUTES	RANGE	PAGE
4	Green Gully & The Dorsal Fin	AM 20min	18	5.8-5.12c	44
5	The White Spot	AM 20min	8	5.10a-5.11c	49
6	Catch The Wave	AM 30min	10	5.9-5.12a	52

This area is the closest to the car when you arrive at the end of Archangel Road. It's often the busiest, with the possible exception of the Monolith, and it includes some great classic climbs such as *Toto, Rebirth, Zulu Warrior, My Pie, Green Lightning* and newer lines *Child Support* and *Riptide Arete*. You are guaranteed to have a great day playing in this area. Drive to the end of Archangel Road and park at the American Alpine Club (AAC) Outhouse. Follow the well-worn trail past the outhouse and across the river. From the river, several trails head to the different areas. Follow the approach descriptions for each area for more information.

The Diamond AM 10min

Approach:
The quickest approach of any of the Hatcher Pass climbing areas located in this book. Park near the American Alpine Club's (AAC) outhouse near the end of Archangel Road. Walk the well-worn path down toward the river; there used to be a cabin here but it burned in 2009. You can cross the river by jumping along on the rocks and the trail continues once on the other side. Walk to the right along the path until you are in line with the buttress, then continue directly up the large boulders. Try to avoid walking on the white boulders as they are still settling.

Area:
There is a plaque on the wall dedicated to the late Steve Garvey who put up many routes in this area and others around the state. The main climb on the wall is *Toto (5.8-5.10b)* which is the classic route of the valley and probably the most climbed route in Hatcher Pass. It's close to the car, has several pitches, and some quality climbing. There are many other routes located on The Diamond that are worth checking out. The majority of the giant rockfall happened 20 years ago (if you were wondering). It should be noted that the top pitches of *Toto* moved around during the 2018 earthquake and became increasingly unstable. If there was a large rockfall from above it is likely that this area could be in the fall zone.

Usually this area gets morning sun and can be out of direct sunlight by late afternoon or early evening. There is loose rock in some areas but most of the well trodden areas of the buttress are solid. The Climbers Alliance of Southcentral Alaska did some great rebuilding of the trail and base of The Diamond. It is important to follow the trail and enjoy the newly made belay ledges without damaging them. If you see something that may need a little bit of attention then help out. It takes the entire community to continue keeping these areas looking great and maintained.

The first two routes are included as a reference and to make sure you know what you're getting in to if you get on them.

1 After Eight 5.5

2 bolts, 3 bolt anchor

I am assuming a portion of this climb has vanished below the depths of rock. There are now only 2 bolts and it is too short to really be a positive climb. The first bolt is also partially crushed. It is the farthest left bolted rock on this face. Any shorter and it would be a boulder problem, I mean a shorter boulder problem.

FA: David Whitelaw, Paul Denkewalter, Charlie Sassara 07.03.1988

2 Psycho 5.9+ ☆

6 bolts, 1 piton, No anchor

Start on the black streak down the low angle slab and climb past 3 bolts. Move right to the more vertical face and climb the horizontal crack with a piton. When I climbed this I didn't see how the middle streak could ever be dry. It was unpleasant and there are no anchors for this climb although records show there used to be a piton anchor that I could not find. Lower off the last bolt, which has a chain, or topout and scramble down.

FA: Skine Boynton, Evan Phillips 2000

3 Twelve O' Clock High 5.10b ☆

Gear to 1", 2 bolt rap anchor

A left leaning corner before another left leaning corner with a chockstone. Climb a crack up into the corner, it doesn't feel so bad yet. Then it gets real ugly. Any hope of a clean crack is dashed. Bring a nut tool and blowtorch to clean out the crack for placements. Climb out and up right to the anchors for *True Grit*.

FA: Steve Garvey, Mike Tumey 1987

4 Hatari 5.10d ☆☆

2 bolts, Gear to 1", 2 bolt rap anchor

Climb left under the small roof and pull over the roof to one bolt. Climb direct to another bolt then find some gear before the hard moves to the anchor. For an easier finish move right to the small cave and climb through an easier crack out.

FA: Steve Garvey

5 True Grit 5.10a ☆☆ 21m

Gear to 3", 2 bolt rap anchor

Climb up left of a slab on vegetation until under the roof. Move right along the crack until it ends then go left into a small cave area. Pull out over the top and walk the grass to the anchor. Has a new anchor, it no longer walks to the anchor for *Hatari*.

FA: Steve Garvey, Jim Sweeney 1987

6 Festoon 5.10a ☆☆☆☆ 21m

2 bolts, Gear to 1", 2 bolt rap anchor

Start on a nice grassy belay ledge and move out right to the seam and a flake tongue. Continue up the flake into a corner. Share anchors with *True Grit*. Originally, this route went left into the small cave area and topped out. The two bolt addition was a separate portion of the climb called *Grit Your Teeth*, which was added later. Easily climbed with a 60m rope.

FA: Jim Sweeney, Steve Garvey 1987

7 Trusting Aborigines 5.11a ☆☆☆

6 bolts, 2 bolt rap anchor

Start low on a wide vegetated crack and climb to a bolted face. Climb over a small lip and continue on vertical dikes. Move left after the 4th bolt to a corner meeting with *Festoon*. Climb the corner to a moss ledge, continue left on the ledge for the same anchor as *True Grit*. You can also climb direct and hook right to meet with the next climb although it is runout and there are no more bolts.

FA: Charlie Sassara, Marty Schmidt 1984

8 Ruby Shoes 5.7, 5.7, 5.7 ☆☆☆☆ **55m**

Pitch 1: 5.7, 1 bolt, Gear to 3", 2 bolt rap anchor 20m
Start up the hill on white rock with a crack which quickly leads to one bolt about 3 meters up. Climb direct then move left to the first anchor. Mossy ledges and loose rock make the first pitch the least enjoyable.
Pitch 2: 5.7, 2 bolts, Gear to 3", 2 bolt rap anchor 20m
Continue moving up and slightly left along the ramp with large blocky holds and 2 bolts in the middle of the route viewable from the belay.
Pitch 3: 5.7, Gear to 3", 2 bolt rap anchor 15m
Move up right on an almost horizontal crack. Continue right until the route meets with *Toto* at a nice deep crack on a slab before the final anchor. All pitches require mostly medium sized cams with a few small thrown in for extra safety. The third pitch is usually skipped and most will rappel from the top of the second.
FA: Dave Staeheli, Lloyd Miller

9 Unknown 5.9, 5.9, 5.7 ☆☆☆ **55m**

Pitch 1: 5.9, 2 bolts, Gear to 3", 2 bolt rap anchor
Starts in a mini corner on white rock up the hill from the arete. First bolt is on top of this small corner. Move right at the first crack which splits the large slab on the right. Continue up and right until a crack which veers left to a bolt. Continue up and left until you are parallel with the anchors. Move right to the anchor.
Pitch 2: 5.9, Gear to 3", 2 bolt rap anchor
Climb up and left into a corner which trends right. Climb along the corner and pull around to the right at the end. Move up to a 2 bolt anchor.
Pitch 3: 5.7, 1 bolt, Gear to 3", 2 bolt rap anchor
Meets with *Toto* for the final pitch. Climb direct to another grassy ledge and move right into a lower angle slab crack. Move up and right to a boulder at the top with bolts for the belay. There is a new bolt in the gully for rappelling; it can be dangerous when wet.

10 Secret Lover 5.10a ☆☆☆

4 bolts, Gear to 2", 2 bolt rap anchor
Start on the lower arete of the buttress with 1 bolt. Continue up the crack to the left side of the arete. Follow a thin seam to a grassy ledge before a face. A fun face climb for this buttress with mostly cracks. Continue staying left of the arete directly to a triangular corner.
FA: Skine Boynton, Raina Panarese 2000

11 Tic Tok 5.8 ☆☆ **35m**

Gear to 3", 2 bolt rap anchor
Start in a mossy corner crack or on the larger crack just left of the corner. Climb direct up over the arete to the south side. Continue on the crack along the corner until parallel with the anchor. Move right to get to the anchors. Originally this route actually moved left to where the anchors for *Secret Lover* are now. It then continued through the open book on a second pitch that has since been claimed by other routes.
FA: Dave Staeheli, Lloyd Miller

12 Toto 5.8, 5.7, 5.8, 5.9+, 5.10a, 5.10a ☆☆☆☆☆

A classic Hatcher Pass climb. Find it on page 37.

13 Auntie M 5.8 ☆☆ **40m**

2 bolts, Gear to 3", 2 bolt rap anchor
Climbs the first 6m of *Toto's* first pitch and then moves right into a large gap. Follow the crack as it moves out of the right corner of the gap. Once the crack leads to the grass move left to use an anchor in the middle of the second pitch of *Toto*. High quality when cleaned.
FA: David Whitelaw, David Freeman 1988

14 The Wizard 5.10b/r ☆☆ **40m**

1 bolt, Gear to 3", 2 bolt rap anchor

Small stoppers and plenty of guts are needed to lead this serious route. Climbs the face 6m right of *Toto* to a large undercling on the face and the only bolt. Four or five meters of crux moves await above the bolt with little gear until meeting with *Auntie M*. Once meeting with *Auntie M* continue to the anchor at the middle of the second pitch of *Toto*. Better to scrub it first.

FA: Scott Woolums, David Whitelaw 1989

15 Nightmare on Diamond Blvd. 5.9

Gear to 4", Slings anchor

Start in the obvious wide off-width chimney overgrown with moss and often wet. Climbs direct onto the ramp at the right. The anchor is a large boulder on the top of the route. Bring long slings to make sure it reaches over the edge. Walkoff the route down the right slope.

FA: Roger Pollard, Tom Evans 1988

16 Emerald Slippers 5.7 ☆☆☆

Gear to 3", Slings anchor

Around right of the formation for *Nightmare on Diamond Blvd.* Climb from the lower edge through thin cracks to a larger crack above and then to a grass area. A large boulder above *Nightmare on Diamond Blvd.* works well for an anchor, bring long slings. Walkoff.

FA: Scott Woolums and friends 1989

Julie Costa on Diversity Hire (p.50)
(Courtesy John Giraldo)

Amos Swanson high
on the Pipeline (p.91)
(Courtesy John Giraldo)

Toto AM 10min

Approach:
Park near the American Alpine Club's (AAC) outhouse and follow the main trail beyond the small cabin toward the creek. Cross the creek and follow the trail as it continues right. It should start going up to the cliff as you come parallel to it. If you cannot find a trail then start walking on large boulders toward the climbs. It is pretty straight forward. Crossing the creek may be the crux of the approach for most people.

Area:
Toto (5.7-5.10b) is a Hatcher Pass classic climb with 6 pitches, although several can be linked easily enough to make it shorter. Located on the The Diamond, it starts just left of the Steve Garvey memorial plaque. Going from the bottom to the top takes about 3-4 hours moving at an average speed but can take a good portion of the day for slower teams. A small portion of this climb used to meander to a part of the rock that is no longer on the wall. A large section of the wall collapsed and areas of the upper wall are still falling. At *Pitch 6 - Pressure Drop (5.10a)* there are other ways you can access the summit, although I am not recommending them. They usually traverse across the ridge along rock that will probably be at the bottom of the valley any day now. The different pitches of this climb will be in the sun at different times of the day.

A Word of Caution: The entire upper buttress was further shaken by the November 2018 earthquake that rattled Anchorage and the surrounding area. This cliff is blocks stacked on blocks, and you can tell by the already significant rockfall that the rest is just waiting to come down. Hopefully this will happen when nobody is around and not while someone is on it. Be aware that several pitches continue to fall apart as the wall degrades. The final pitches are no longer recommended for climbing.

6
5
4
3
2
1
Summit
5.10a
5.7
5.10a
5.10b
5.9
5.9
5.10b
5.8
5.7
5.8
Garvey Memorial Plaque

Each pitch variation is listed from left to right on the face.

1 Pitch 1 5.8 ☆☆☆☆
Gear to 3", 2 bolt rap anchor
Start just left of the Steve Garvey memorial plaque and climb up a nice large crack. Move slightly left to a belay ledge.

2 Pitch 2 5.7 ☆☆☆
2 bolts, Gear to 3", 2 bolt rap anchor
Climb up to a grassy ledge and move right into a lower angle slab crack. There is a 2 bolt intermediate anchor on this pitch but is easy to skip. Move up and right to a boulder at the top with bolts for the belay. There is a decent walkoff along the right ramp from here if you choose to descend and not continue along the upper pitches. There is a single bolt high left for the retreat or some short scrambling.

3 Pitch 3 5.8 ☆☆
5 bolts, Gear to 3", 3 bolt rap anchor
From the boulder above *Pitch 2,* climb up the moss to a prominent arete. The first two bolts are close enough to be a belay anchor. Follow the arete which has a few bolts to another grass ledge. Climb the grass up right to the anchors below the crack.

4 Pitch 4 - Thin Crack Var. 5.9+ ☆☆☆☆
Gear to 1", 2 bolt rap anchor
Climb direct of the anchors into a sharp but enjoyable corner crack. Walk right once at the top of the crack to the anchors which are above the off-width.

4 Pitch 4 - Bestiality 5.10b ☆☆☆☆
Gear to 4", 2 bolt rap anchor
Climb right of the anchors up a deep crack to another ledge then jump into the off-width. Mandatory 4" cam. Widens at the top before going to the anchor. So called because of a reported Garvey comment, "because it's like humping the dog."
FA: Jim Sweeney, Mike Tumey 1990

5 Pitch 5 - AAA Arete 5.10b 💣
12 bolts, 2 bolt rap anchor
Walk or be lowered from the *Pitch 4 - Bestiality* anchors down the ramp and around the cliff to a section of the wall which used to exist. The start of this variation has since disappeared and the bottom two bolts of this section were crushed when the rock wall fell. Instead, there is another possible way to get to this climb which is recommended if you are going up the bolted section. Climb up the slab to two bolts and move left to the arete. There is a runout here with a possible nasty fall before meeting with this route which is on the face left around the arete. Climb direct on bolts to the anchor.
FA: Steve Garvey, Jim Sweeney

5 Pitch 5 - Crack Var. 5.10a ☆☆☆☆
1 piton, Gear to 4", 2 bolt rap anchor
Not easy to miss once at the anchors for *Pitch 4 - Bestiality*. Climb easy ground to the harder looking section of this arm / hands crack. Bring plenty of 3" cams and a few 4" wouldn't hurt. At the top of the crack veer left under the roof and pull out right once at the arete. Use runners to avoid some serious rope drag to the anchors.

5 Pitch 5 - Right Escape Var. 5.9 ☆☆
1 bolt, Gear to 1", 2 bolt rap anchor
From the anchor on the ledge above *Bestiality* this variation can be easy to miss. Walk along the slab to the right toward the drop-off. There should be one bolt about head height. Clip the bolt and pull around the corner to the right getting some instant exposure. This is the best part of this pitch. After pulling the crack continue on easier climbing toward the top of the cliff. You should find an anchor on a grassy ledge above. Watch for loose rocks on this pitch as they would take out anyone taking the rappel gully from *Pitch 3.*

6 Pitch 6 - Pressure Drop 5.10a/r 💣
2 bolts, 2 piton, Gear to 2", 2 bolt anchor
It is recommended that you skip this pitch due to shifting from the Nov. 2018 earthquake. From the anchors of *Pitch 5 - Crack Var.* walk right down the slope to the rock wall with horizontal cracks. Start on the arete of that wall to the left of a small roof. Climb the arete through cracks to 1 piton below the roof. Pull through the lip using a new bolt and follow the slab on bolts and pitons to a thin crack that has some tricky gear. Don't forget to bring your stoppers. Once above the slab climb up grassy ledges to the anchor at the summit of the buttress.
FA: Zach Shlosar, Eric Mize

6 Pitch 6 - Crakken Chimney 5.7 💣
Toprope, 2 bolt anchor
This pitch is best toproped as it climbs a large chimney that is not currently protectable. From the summit of Toto rappel back down the face as for *Pressure Drop* but keep to the right and you'll see the chimney. It is best to be lowered from above and climb out. There is a big grass ledge where you can start the pitch.

Zulu Wall AM 10min

Approach:
Park near the American Alpine Club's (AAC) outhouse and hike the well-worn trail to the boulder crossing over the creek. Continue right on the trail until at the far right end of Zulu Wall. Follow the trail which leads toward the wall and goes along the base. You can also approach from The Diamond if you wish to go there first, and that may be a faster way to go when heading direct for *Zulu Warrior (5.10b/r)* and the climbs on the left side of the wall.

Area:
A little bit of everything is found in this area. Stemming on vertical dikes, overhanging vertical cracks, and bolted slab; it's a pleasurable experience spending a day at the Zulu Wall. This wall has some great routes including *Zulu Warrior (5.10b/r)* and *Voodoo Child (5.10b/r)* which are excellent quality bolted slab routes. They can be serious leads, especially *Zulu Warrior*, where the bolts are often runout with sizeable gaps between. A fall clipping any of these bolts would lead to some rather painful bouncing and could end in injury. It is also important to remember that many of these routes will stretch a 60m rope, and depending where you stand on the slope, you could find yourself being lowered off the end of the rope.

When I was climbing in Red Rocks, Nevada I mentioned to a group next to us that I was from Alaska. The belayer for the other group started to tell me about how the climbing guide for Alaska was wrong and how bad it was. I believe he had climbed *Zulu Warrior* or *Root 66*. He then joked, "But you didn't write it....did you?" When I didn't say anything he realized that I had. It was a fun experience that we both laughed about. The guide may not always be correct, it is up to you to take the necessary precautions to stay safe (I had written the height correct but it was not easy to see).

Watch out for falling rock on the left side of the wall if there are parties on the summit pitches of *Toto (5.7-5.10b)*. There is not a whole lot of rock left on this wall so it doesn't see much development these days.

1 Bowl of Stones 5.10a ☆☆

4 bolts, Gear to 1", 3 bolt anchor
Hard start and harder for anyone not 6 ft. tall. Begin in a small cave overhang and meander the face to just before a mass of broken rocks. Bring some gear to eliminate the runouts.
FA: John Trautwein, David Whitelaw, Amy Johnson 1989

2 Unknown 5.9, 5.10c 💣 — 50m

NOT RECOMMENDED
Pitch 1: 5.9, Gear to 3", 2 bolt anchor — 20m
Above the previous route is a bunch of "spaghettio" rocks ready to fall, and above that is this climb. Scramble to a wide dirty crack and climb up to a slab with a belay anchor below the arete. This climb is in the *Toto* death zone! The anchor is too crushed to get webbing through, so new bolts are needed before this becomes a viable climb again. Also, don't climb if there is anyone on *Toto* above or *Zulu Wall* below.
Pitch 2: 5.10c, 11 bolts, Slings anchor — 30m
Climb up left into a corner and traverse right to the arete. Continue on the arete to the top. Walk on loose rocks and find a good place to belay without killing your belayer. BEWARE!
FA: Steve Garvey, Paul Wharton

3 Voodo Child 5.10b/r ☆☆☆☆☆ — 2

5 bolts, Gear to .5", 2 bolt rap anchor
Begin on a crack which goes up and left before moving right at around 8 meters. Moves right to share anchors with *Zulu Warrior*.
FA: Evan Smith, David Miller 1985

4 Zulu Warrior 5.10b/r ☆☆☆☆☆ — 30m

5 bolts, Gear to .5", 2 bolt rap anchor
Start on a right angling crack with an indent in the rock at ground level. Place some pieces here up to .5" but don't expect any between the bolts. Stemming on vertical dikes in the rock make this an oddly enjoyable experience. Move right or left of the bulge before the topout to the anchors. Classic.
FA: Evan Smith, David Miller 1985

5 Root 66 5.10a ☆☆☆ — 35m

Gear to 1", 2 bolt rap anchor
Start on a slab that leads up to a corner crack. Climb onto the top of the corner and move right along ledges to a flake (which sounds like it's ready to go). Place pro on the flake if you are daring enough, then climb corners with good placements to the top. Pull over the top of the crack system to a grass ledge. Walk left along the ledge to the anchors.
FA: Roger Pollard, Mark Jewell, Kenji Seta, Randy Zernzach 1987

Tower 5.12c ☆☆☆

, Gear to 1", 2 bolt anchor

w in a corner and climb up a bolted blank slab onto a ledge. Move up and left of the roof and through cracks on gear until the corner. Pull over the lip for the anchor.

FA: Paul Turecki, Steve Garvey

7 Right Trident Crack 5.11+ ☆☆☆

1 bolt, Gear to 3", 2 bolt anchor

Climb / scramble to the base of this slightly overhanging roof. Climb toward the center crack where there is one bolt on the lower slab. Move into the overhanging crack and climb direct. Bring slings for the anchor.

FA: Paul Turecki

8 Physical Attraction 5.8 ☆☆☆☆☆

Gear to 1", 2 bolt rap anchor

Start on a good grassy ledge and walk into the corner. Begin on the obvious corner crack. This climb is down and right of the slightly overhanging roof with many cracks.

FA: Dave Nyman, Jim Sweeney 1987

9 Willing 5.9 ☆☆☆

Gear to 2", 2 bolt rap anchor

Start up grass ledges 3 meters right of *Physical Attraction* and follow broken cracks to the same anchor. The crux comes right at the end.

FA: Dave Nyman, Jim Sweeney 1988

10 Role Model 5.9r ☆☆

3 bolts, 2 bolt rap anchor

Scramble up a few mossy ledges to the slabby arete of this portion of the wall. Climb on the slab staying right of the corner with an often wet crack to the top of a big ledge. Move immediately left of the ledge to another face with 1 bolt.

FA: David Whitelaw, Greg Bombeck 1988

11 If I Should Stumble 5.6 ☆☆

Gear to 2", 2 bolt rap anchor

On the far right side walk up a gully to a square section of rock with blocks and cracks. Climbing the right side of this block will stay around 5.6. Climbing the center of the block is also fun and goes between 5.9-5.10a.

FA: David Skidmore, Eric

12 Linear Adventure 5.8 ☆☆☆

Gear to 3", 2 bolt rap anchor

Climb up a shattered face which goes to a small grass ledge then continues to a second larger grass ledge. Move left at the second ledge to a seam / crack before the ledge ends. Climb up the seam and move right at the finish for the anchors.

FA: David Whitelaw, Greg Bombeck

13 Blockheads 5.7 ☆☆☆

1 bolt, Gear to 3", 2 bolt rap anchor

Climb the same start as *Linear Adventure* and move right along the second ledge to a bolt. From the bolt climb the crack direct through the slab.

FA: David Whitelaw, Amy Johnson 1988

14 Odorono 5.9 ☆☆

3 bolts, Gear to 2", 2 bolt rap anchor

To access this climb walk up and left of *Linear Adventure* to the corner. Scramble up dirty 5.4 climbing to another grassy area. Walk around to the base of the slab with bolts in it. Climb 3 bolts on the slab then choose your direction along the face. The further you move left the more you will have to come right for anchors which are on the right above the climb. Scramble back down the 5.4 or walkoff the top of the climb for the descent.

FA: Amy Johnson, David Whitelaw 1988

Lexi Trainer climbing Physical Attraction. It's all smiles on the Zulu Wall. (Courtesy John Borland / morffed.com)

Eliza Stokes climbing Voodoo Child, a classic slab / face route at Zulu Wall. (Courtesy John Borland / morffed.com)

Green Gully & The Dorsal Fin AM 20min

Approach:

Park near the American Alpine Club's (AAC) outhouse and walk toward the river. Cross the river on the boulders and continue direct to the upper rock band; moving right on the trail brings you to *Toto (5.7-5.10a)* and Zulu Wall. Walk along boulders and head right up the first gully full of grass. Most of the routes are halfway up the gully. The Green Gully climbs are on the main wall. The Dorsal Fin is a section of rock that juts out between the Green Gully and the fallen gully. **DO NOT** go up the gully with the white colored rock. That area fell within the last 15-20 years and is still loose.

Area:

Most of the routes here are hard and fun. This area has great potential for more climbing especially above the main wall and further up the gully. The top of the gully has seen climbing for years but only recently became a trade area. The climbs in the upper gully such as *My Pie (5.11b)* and *Green Lightning (5.10c)* are destined to see plenty of traffic in the coming years as they are excellent well protected routes. Climbs such as *Unknown 420 (5.10+)* will probably see less traffic due to being an adventure route but that shouldn't stop you from checking it out anyway. The beauty of Hatcher Pass is exploration and a sense of adventure. As routes become "safer" with bolts and bolted anchors, it's important to remember that these routes shouldn't be relics of time but objectives awaiting the next bold individual.

1 The Grow Room 5.4, 5.11a, 5.10d ☆☆☆ 42m

Pitch 1: 5.4, Gear to 3", 2 bolt anchor

An access pitch to get to the good stuff. Climb a pitch of mixed grass and rock to get to the first anchor in the corner.

Pitch 2: 5.11a, 1 piton, Gear to 4", 2 bolt anchor

Move right and follow the slab using old an old piton then head toward the large overhang. Go through the steep left side and belay below the splitters above.

Pitch 3: 5.10d, Gear to 3", 2 bolt rap anchor

Climb a short splitter to an anchor. This pitch can be linked with the second pitch depending on rope drag.

FA: Ben Chriswell, Elliott Gaddy 2019

2 Prelude to Aid 5.10c, 5.12 ☆☆☆ **40m**

Pitch 1: 5.10c, 1 bolt, 2 pitons, Gear to 1", 2 bolt anchor

Scramble up to a grass ledge and climb into a corner. Harder moves than probably expected with a few pitons, then move left to the anchor. This first pitch was climbed by Steve Garvey and Paul Wharton. They tried to aid toward the right but found that the rock was loose and crumbly. They finished here and the second pitch was added later by a different party who took the route more direct.

FA: Steve Garvey, Paul Wharton

Pitch 2: 5.12, 4 bolts, 2 pitons, Gear to .5", 2 bolt anchor

Climb direct to a hard face, smear and hope it sticks through hard moves with a few bolts. The anchor is just below the roof.

FA: Paul Turecki, Bob Kohut 1995

3 Dark Light 5.12 ☆

1 bolt, 2 pitons, Gear to 1", No anchor

Climb the first pitch of *Prelude to Aid* and move right of the anchors to a bolt. Move across the face to a crack with a piton then head up to a piton below the roof.

FA: Paul Turecki, Bob Kohut 1994

4 White Spot Roofs 5.10a, 5.11c, 5.10d ☆☆☆☆ **45m**

Pitch 1: 5.10a, Gear to 3", 2 bolt anchor

Climb either left or right up to the anchors. Climbing up left will include grass and vegetation while the rock on the right is more solid.

Pitch 2: 5.11c, 5 bolts, Gear to 2", 2 bolt anchor

The cracks are as good as they look and take plenty of gear. Pulling over them is indeed the hard part but worth the effort. Bolts along the way make this route feel well protected but stoppers are also very helpful.

Pitch 3: 5.10d, 4+ bolts, Gear to 2", 2 bolt anchor

Climb right of the belay onto a face. Continue into a corner, move right to the anchors. Double rope rappel.

5 The Brown Spot 5.11d ☆☆☆ **35m**

Gear to 2", 3 bolt anchor

Start just right of a face 1 meter before *Unknown #6*. Climb a flake toward a piton not seen from the ground, then hook left onto a small ledge with a thin seam. There is a fixed piton to protect the crux here and some small TCU cams would help in the seam. After pulling past the seam it opens to a crack with a lieback, finger and face goodness to the anchor. Bring two 0 and two 00 cams. Primarily small gear. Double rope rappel.

FA: Andy Hoyt 06.2008

6 Unknown 5.9+, 5.9 ☆☆☆☆ 40m

Pitch 1: 5.9+, Gear to 3", 2 bolt anchor ☆☆☆☆☆ 28m

Begins in a shattered crack just right of a blank face and left of a face slab. Climb the crack to a small roof through great hand and fist jams to the first anchor. Bring plenty of cams around the 2" range.

Pitch 2: 5.9, Gear to 3", 3 bolt anchor ☆☆ 12m

Climb up about two meters beyond the anchors then veer left along loose blocks to a ledge. Go direct up the crack from the ledge and the anchors are on the left. Bring slings to help eliminate rope drag.

FA: Paul Turecki, Bob Kohut

7 Unknown 5.8 ☆ 30m

Gear to 3", 1 bolt + 1 piton anchor

Just right of the previous route. Climb the first few feet of the previous route then move right onto dirt and loose blocks. Continue right until going up a corner to the anchor. There is an abundance of loose rock.

Unknown #6 is probably one of the best 5.9 gear leads around. Great climbing leads you through a roof and to the anchor. The second pitch isn't really worth it but it is good access if you want to toprope The Brown Spot.

8 Danger Maus 5.11+ ☆☆☆☆

1 bolt, Gear to .5", 2 bolt anchor

Fifteen meters uphill from the other climbs, this one moves up a green streak and a clean face to one bolt. A recommended (or necessary) all points off dyno will get you past the first crux. Continue through gear that can be hard to find.

FA: Ben Chriswell, Aaron Thrasher 2011

9 Unknown 420 5.10+ ☆☆☆

Gear to 4", Gear anchors

This is one of those unfortunate routes that missed getting into this book in its entirety. I've read everything from, "best multipitch crack climb in the area" to "it's not bad" to "chossy." Either way it's an adventure. The upper pitches are ones that many have wondered about. A large crack/chimney in a corner that leads up to a large block split by a crack through the gray rock. The first pitch is a moss scramble at 5.7 and then the second pitch starts right into a crack dihedral. Move left to the base of the large chimney and from the top of the chimney head left to find the white face and steep crack. Ends on a ledge above. There are said to be rappel anchors off route.

FA: Just Another Stoner

10 Hot Laps 5.7, 5.10a ☆☆☆

Pitch 1: 5.7, Gear to 3", 2 bolt anchor

The best way to get to this climb is to begin on the grass ledge as you would for *Green Lightning* and walk the grass left until you are under a long corner with an anchor under a small roof at the end. Climb the corner.

Pitch 2: 5.10a, Gear to 3", 2 bolt anchor

Climb out left of the corner and then up to a roof split by a wide crack. The anchor is just below the roof. Double rope rappel back to the start.

FA: Austin Thayer, Paul Wharton

11 The Green Snake 5.10+ PG13 ☆☆☆½ 33m

1 piton, Gear to 2", 2 bolt rap anchor

This climb is located directly below *My Pie* and starts off a grass ledge with a 2 bolt belay anchor. Scramble across to the anchor from high in the gully. Start easy then climb a seam with thin gear. You'll want brass nuts, offset cams, and small gear of all types as well as selection of other cams. Cleaned by Ben Chriswell and Chris Williams.

FA: Amos Swanson

Bonus: There is a traverse route that is called Toto to Pinnacle. You start by climbing Toto to the top and then traversing along the ridge until you come to the area in the picture below. Those wanting the full experience can climb Green Lightning to My Pie and then continue on the ridge to finally top out on The Pinnacle. It's a big day and should only be attempted by experienced parties; loose rock abounds.

12 Green Lightning 5.5, 5.10c ☆☆☆☆☆ **50m**

Pitch 1: 5.5, Gear to 2", 2 bolt anchor *20m*

Start up the grass and follow thin cracks on the slab to make a gear anchor at the base of the goods. This pitch also splits to the left and goes up a thin seam toward the first pitch anchor of *My Pie* and the top of the second pitch for *Green Lightning*. Climbing that direction is considered the first pitch of *Rebecca's Roof*.

Pitch 2: 5.10c, 3 pitons, Gear to 3", 2 bolt rap anchor *30m*

Put on your happy face and get right to the crux of the pitch. Place some gear quick as a fall to the slab would be painful. Avoid placing gear on the block. Head left on the crack that shoots to the anchor. There are fixed pitons on sparse gear sections. For the descent it is best to do a double rope rappel back to the ground or a 35m rappel back to a ledge where you can scramble to the ground. The ledge below is a full 35m so a 70m rope will just make it. Tie knots in the end!

FA: Ben Chriswell, Zach Shlosar, Skine Boynton

13 My Pie 5.10b / 5.11b ☆☆☆☆☆ **18m**

Gear to 4", 2 bolt rap anchor

This is possibly the best crack of its grade in Hatcher. It is almost certainly the closest to the road and most easily accessible. There are two variations to the finger crack section. I'll list them here, but I can't tell you how to eat your pie. The gear for each variation is similar requiring small gear.

To get to the base of the climb you can do the first pitch of *Rebecca's Roof* at 5.9, or to get the best two pitches around combine it with *Green Lightning*. From the belay anchor, head directly left onto some big blocks, climbing carefully up to the base of the *Pie*.

Left Var. : 5.10b - Excellent finger locks lead to hand jams and back to a few locks before one final fun move and the top.

Right Var. : 5.11b - In case you were feeling like the left side was too easy, the right variation starts tricky and gives you the crux right before the rest. Hand jams and some more fingers to the top. Pick either side, they're both excellent.

For the descent, it is best to rappel back to the belay anchor and then do a double rope rappel back to the ground or a 35m rappel back to a ledge where you can scramble to the ground. The ledge below is a full 35m so a 70m rope will just make it. Tie knots in the end!

FA: Skine Boynton, Zach Shlosar

14 Rebecca's Roof 5.9, 5.12c ☆☆☆ **56m**

Pitch 1: 5.9, Gear to 2", 2 bolt anchor *40m*

Scramble up grass and small ledges until you are on a slab below *Green Lightning*. From the slab, traverse left using small cracks for gear until a slabby corner. Climb directly toward the roof. There is a belay anchor for the short second pitch on a ledge.

Pitch 2: 5.12c, Gear to 4", 2 bolt rap anchor *16m*

Bring RP's and a #4 BD cam for this pitch, which includes small gear, a slung pod, and climbing in a flare through steep ground. To descend, you can bring two ropes and do a long rappel from the top of the roof or rappel back to the first pitch anchor and do a 35m rappel back to a grass ledge. It takes every inch of a 70m rope to get back to the lower ledge. Scramble off the ledge to the right and back to the start.

FA: Aaron Thrasher, Ben Chriswell, Josh Varney

The next climbs are located on The Dorsal Fin which is on the right side of the main gully.

15 Makin' Hole 5.10c ☆☆☆☆ **30m**

9 bolts, 2 pitons, 2 bolt anchor

Climb the slab with a small lip at the bottom over easy chickenhead climbing. Move left at the first ledge to the second slab face. Climb harder moves meandering around the bolt line to the top. Bring a M/L cam for the lower section to eliminate a runout on easy ground.

FA: Steve Garvey, Paul Wharton

These 3 climbs are on a small slab of rock that is known as the After Eight Slab. It gets very little traffic but has a few enjoyable climbs. Due to the instability of the rocks it is still recommended that you avoid walking on the large talus blocks, especially those that are still white. A 60m rope works for all three routes.

16 Unknown 5.8 ☆☆

Gear to 1", 2 bolt anchor

Climb the crack from the left and meet with the main route before the anchor. Sometimes awkward to find gear.

17 Unknown 5.10c ☆☆☆

2 bolts, 1 piton, Gear to 1", 2 bolt anchor

Climb a black streak on the left side for a direct start. Hard moves all the way to the first bolt. Watch for loose flakes at the top.

18 After That 5.10c ☆☆☆

Toprope, 2 bolt anchor

Start on the right crack and move straight up the face. Meet with the previous route before the anchor. Also a good way to approach the first bolt of the previous route.

The White Spot AM 20min

Approach:

This wall is the last in the Lower Webfoot Area before curving up the valley and heading for other walls such as the Lost Wall. Start at the American Alpine Club's (AAC) outhouse and walk the well-worn trail to the river. Cross at the boulders and continue direct toward the cliff instead of hooking right. Continue through the boulder field and head directly toward the left end of the rock band ahead. When you are approaching the valley on the road, this wall looks like a giant diamond. Avoid the white rocks as much possible.

Area:

Portions of this wall seem to remain wet during the summer. *Waves of Pleasure (5.11c)* is a good example of this since it drips for most the year except when frozen. There is a cave where one can hide from the rain if it starts to come down heavy. This area originally included the *White Spot Roofs (5.11c)* and surrounding routes, but they have since been split into the Green Gully and the Dorsal Fin. There are routes located all over this wall and the upper faces. There is a route that goes up the main portion of the face for 3-4 pitches and is called The White Spot. According to Jim Sweeney the final pitch of this route is NOT recommended due to many portions of loose rock; it would end at the gully for Catch the Wave.

This wall has seen a resurgence lately, mainly due to new bolts and new routes. Many of the bolts and anchors have been replaced with several of the routes getting new starts or cleaned cracks. The addition of *Child Support (5.11a)* has also increased the areas popularity as it gets high praise. The second pitch is likely one of the best well bolted sport pitches around.

1 Waves of Pleasure 5.11c ☆☆☆☆ 45m

12 bolts, Gear to 2", 2 bolt rap anchor

Mostly a bolted climb. Start on the featured face with cracks and climb to the right of the roof. Climb on slab then a crack to the next small roof. Continue on slab and chickenheads as it moves right to the anchor. Double rope rappel; a walkoff is possible but not recommended.

FA: Paul Turecki

2 Diversity Hire 5.10c ☆☆☆☆ 35m

7 bolts, Gear to 2", 2 bolt rap anchor

This new climb starts just to the right of *Waves of Pleasure* and follows a shallow corner using gear. Several small roofs with bolts lead you through a final bulge before the anchor. A .75" cam works good here. Primarily thin gear and is fairly well protected for those who know how to place small gear.

FA: Chris Williams, Tom Myhre 08.2020

Anyone who has the previous rock climbing guide may notice some changes to these routes. As routes are cleaned and rebolted they occasionally change or redirect. With the new changes these climbs should see a lot more traffic, this area is excellent and should not be ignored. Bring a 70m rope!

3 Fairwell Transmission 5.10b/c ☆☆☆ 35m

7 bolts, Gear to .75", 1 piton, 2 bolt rap anchor

There are places for gear before the first bolt. Start on the slab and climb a broken thin crack to ledges and the first bolt. Climb direct to a grass ledge and move left at the ledge to climb to another larger grass ledge. Move left to use the same anchor as *Diversity Hire* to skip the grass topout. This route and the next two can be done with a single 60m rope but it usually requires very careful belaying and some downclimbing. It is best to use a 70m rope for the climbs on this face.

FA: Roger Pollard, Jim Sweeney

4 Better Things 5.10a ☆☆☆☆☆ 36m

13 bolts, 2 bolt rap anchor

Start low on this wonderfully featured slab. First bolt is 3 meters up. There is a runout here between the first and second bolt where you could place a cam if necessary; otherwise the route is closely bolted. Route goes right until the arete then follows direct and crosses the often wet moss another 5 meters to the anchors, which can be hard to see if you are not yet on the grass ledge.

FA: Steve Garvey, Paul Wharton

5 Dead End 5.10b ☆☆ **36m**
8 bolts, Gear to 1", 2 bolt rap anchor
Start low on the slab before a corner and climb easy holds to the face on the right. There is a single bolt on the face. Move direct to a grass ledge. Pro can be used for this lower portion or you can traverse from the first bolt of *Better Things* and move right to meet with this climb. Move into a bolted corner and onto another nice ledge where the climb meets with *Better Things*. Move direct to the large grass ledge with the anchors which are hard to see.
FA: Steve Garvey, Eddie Phay

6 Deadbeat Dad 5.10b, 5.11a ☆☆☆☆ **61m**
Pitch 1: 5.10b, 7 bolts, Gear to 2", 2 bolt anchor *31m*
Start low in a crack with flakes. Move direct on gear to the roof. Continues on bolts for the rest of the climb. Climb direct onto a slabby ledge which can be a bit ugly to get on top of.
Pitch 2: 5.11a, 8 bolts, 2 bolt anchor *28m*
Climb left of the belay and up right again to the arete. Follow the arete over a bulge crux before a ledge. Getting on top of the next ledge can be an oddity. Move left along the ledge to a better place to pull on the grass, which often remains wet. Walk a few meters along the sloped grass ledge to the anchor.
FA: Steve Garvey, Jim Sweeney

7 Child Support 5.10b/c, 5.11a ☆☆☆☆☆ **65m**
Pitch 1: 5.10b/c, 3 bolts, Gear to 2", 2 bolt rap anchor *35m*
Climbs the right line of two trad starts. Easy climbing up to just before the first bolt. Follow up the slab to another bolt and through the roof. A shallow corner leads you to the traverse right on big holds. Another thin crack leads you to the finish. Tie knots in the end of your rope, it is a long rappel.
Pitch 2: 5.11a, 13 bolts, 2 bolt rap anchor *30m*
The first bolt is a ways out and a BD .75 can be used to fill the gap. Excellent climbing on thin holds up the face. Very well bolted; be ready to stand on your toes. Shares an anchor with *Deadbeat Dad*.
FA: Ben Chriswell, Chris Williams, Lang Van Dommelen, Julie Costa

8 Blueberry Crack 5.11c ☆☆☆☆
Gear to 5", 1 bolt + Gear anchor
Who says you have to walk a long way to get your offwidth fix? This steep difficult climb is at the base of green gully and just around the corner from *Deadbeat Dad*. Climb a steep section into the widening crack with a steep mantle finish.
FA: Aaron Thrasher, Ben Chriswell

Regan Marin climbing Child Support.

Catch the Wave AM 30min

Approach:
Park at the American Alpine Club's (AAC) outhouse or nearby and walk the well trodden trail toward the river. Cross the creek by hopping boulders. There is an intermittent trail which travels to the base of The White Spot and if you can find it that is the one to take. Otherwise take a direct route along boulders and tundra toward the wall. Once at The White Spot move left along the cliff base on a trail that curves around the cliff and right. Once you have passed the cliff, walk immediately right up a grass gully staying on the grass portion. Continue to the ridge where you can hook left onto a large grass ledge where the main climbs are located.

Area:
Since this area is tucked away behind The White Spot and The Diamond it does not see as much traffic, which is unfortunate because of the quality of the routes. If you wish to get away from others but not have to hike too far, head up to the Catch the Wave wall. There is a lot of potential in this area and there are some routes that are not listed in this guide. This would be an excellent place to explore for the day.

There are several new routes in this section from the previous guidebook edition. This includes an older route called *Gateway (5.9)* and the surrounding climbs. These pitches were included in the original guidebook called First Steps and, while they saw the occasional ascent, have not had a lot of traffic over the years. That changed recently when they started to get posted online and it is now more common to see climbers up on the hillside. These climbs are enjoyable old-school Hatcher style ascents, currently without bolted anchors and with plenty of moss wrangling.

Riptide Arete (5.12a) adds to the upper wall that has an already excellent concentration of high quality routes, including *Rebirth (5.11c)*, which is one of the best cracks in the valley.

While the first few climbs in this chapter are just now making it into the guide, they are some of the original routes on the wall. They also appear to be shedding some rock, as is common in Alaska. Approach with care and always be weary of loose blocks / flakes.

1 Gateway 5.6, 5.6r, 5.9 ☆☆☆☆ 134m

Pitch 1: 5.6, Gear to 4", Gear Anchor ☆☆ 50m

There are several variations to this pitch up to 5.8. There are multiple short crack systems that can be climbed onto a grass ledge; you then walk the grass ledges for a while until a large flat ledge. This pitch is usually just skipped by walking in from the right along a thin grass ramp. Walk up the gully toward Catch the Wave, looking for a grass ramp going to the left along the cliff. If wet, it can feel more dangerous. This is also the descent line.

Pitch 2: 5.6r, Gear to 2", Gear anchor ☆ 50m

This pitch definitely has a reputation for being the most annoying part of the route. When dry, it's not too bad, if you're accustomed to Hatcher Pass moss scrambles. Pick your best line along the grass ramps, connecting rock bands with intermittent gear until below the cracks above. Gear can be hard to find. Using your hand as a claw tends to work well.

Pitch 3: 5.9, Gear to 5", Slings anchor ☆☆☆☆ 34m

You finally made it! Most parties can get by with only one BD #4 and one BD #5 or comparable cam. Follow the left hands / fist crack that goes around the corner. After pulling the corner it turns into great fingers and then back to wide. Move right at the top to use the slung horn. Shares the slings anchor with the next routes. Bring slings in case it needs replacing. A 30m rappel gets you back to the ledge.

Descent: You will need to rappel old slings slung around horns. Bring material to replace just in case of damage or if they are old. Never trust someone else's old tat. From the top, rappel back to a slung horn at the base of *Chim-knee*. Rappel back to the large ledge using two ropes. There is another anchor on this rappel; it should be on your right-hand side. This anchor could allow you to breakup the rap to be able to rappel with one 70m rope. Best to bring two ropes. From the large grass ledge, walk right along the cliff edge back to the approach trail for Catch the Wave.

2 Chim-knee 5.9 ☆☆ 30m

Gear to 3", Slings anchor

In the back of the detached flake, the right side of which is *Offwide*. This climb is usually toproped, gear can be difficult to find and there are large blocks inside of the chimney. Usually toproped. Descend the same as *Gateway*.

3 Offwide 5.8 ☆☆☆☆ **31m**
Gear to 4", Slings anchor
Doing just one of the climbs on this ledge may not feel like it was worth the trouble but thankfully there are a few enjoyable lines. Start on thin cracks with good gear, head up into the wide crack that thins as you go higher. Fun climbing and plenty of placements for large gear. Bring several of the larger sizes to protect this one well, a BD #5 may be helpful but can be avoided.

4 Slab Trek 5.11, 5.11+, 5.12 / 5.13 ☆☆☆
Pitch 1: 5.11, Trad rack, 3 bolt anchor
Start low in the gully below the large slab with a very obvious roof half way up the wall. Probably the most defined feature of the area. Climb through blocks and moss onto an anchor before the large slab. The crux move is getting over a short block in a small roof. There are a few fixed pitons on this pitch and I've heard it's an involved climb on its own.
Pitch 2: 5.11+, Trad rack, 2 bolt anchor
From the anchor traverse right along a mossy crack. The gear is well spaced along this traverse with few areas for pro. Continue all the way right to the corner. Follow the corner toward the large roof and an anchor.
FA: Steve Garvey, Paul Wharton
Pitch 3: 5.12, Trad rack, 2 bolt anchor
This pitch was added later by a different party. Move up and right into the dihedral on the slab then traverse left across the underside of the roof until the crack. Pull through the crack and follow as it meanders left and ends. TCU's mandatory for the roof.
Pitch 3 Var. 1 - Project: 5.13, bolts, 2 bolt anchor
This bolted slab was put up by Aaron Thrasher and has yet to be climbed clean.

5 Rebirth 5.11c ☆☆☆☆☆ **30m**
Gear to 3", 2 bolt rap anchor
Start climbing toward a great looking corner. Climb on a wide flake until the large roof. Move left along the upper crack and work your way out of the roof. There is a new 2 bolt anchor once you exit the squeeze; you are no longer required to use the old pitons or hike to the anchor for *Cheese Pit Blues*. A BD #5 is optional at the beginning. Classic!
FA: Steve Garvey

6 The Prospect 5.11c ☆☆☆ **35m**
2 bolts, Gear to 3", 2 bolt rap anchor
Start in a thin crack just right of the corner arete. Climb direct to the hard slab moves and 2 bolts. Continue slightly left into a wider crack. Move direct to the finish. Walk a mossy ramp to the anchor for *Cornish Head*.
FA: Steve Garvey, Paul Wharton

7 Cheese Pit Blues 5.10b ☆☆☆☆ **35m**
1 piton, Gear to 4", 2 bolt rap anchor
Start in a corner and follow an excellent crack to the finish. Has some occasional crumble and could use more traffic. Lieback, fingers, and body wedge your way up.
FA: Steve Garvey, Mark Yerkes 1988

8 Cornish Head 5.10a ☆☆☆ **38m**
4 bolts, 1 piton, Gear to 1", 2 bolt rap anchor
Route continues on a leftward angle to the anchors. After the 3rd bolt, climb the corner to a small roof and move left onto the slab. Bring two ropes for the rappel.
FA: Steve Garvey, Paul Wharton 1987

Amos Swanson climbing into the goods on Rebirth. (Courtesy Caleb Helkenn)

9 The Last Resort 5.9 ☆☆☆ 15m

Gear to 3", 2 bolt rap anchor

Begin just left of the humongous block that contains *Riptide Arete*. Climb through a roof, watch for some loose horns and blocks after the roof on the right hand side, and move left along a grassy ledge. There is a 2 bolt rap anchor on this ledge now that was added later that can be used as a belay or to lower back to the ground. The route used to continue beyond but it has become increasingly unstable and is not really that enjoyable past the anchor anyway. Best to lower here. *Extension Var. 5.7:* Going direct from here takes you through loose blocks (one normally slung) and onto a ledge where you can walk / scramble left across ledges to the anchors for *Cornish Head*. Sling a block on top to belay from above this portion of the route. To continue on the original route, move up and left of the bolted anchor to a wide open flake with a terrifying boulder precariously wedged within. Climb out and onto the grass ledge. Move up left for the anchor for *Cornish Head*. (40m)

FA: Paul Wharton, Steve Garvey 1988

10 Riptide Arete 5.12a ☆☆☆☆☆ 24m

5 bolts, Gear to 2", 2 bolt rap anchor

Ascends the arete in an amazing position. Follow clean cracks up to a few bolts and then on to the ledge. Climb orange rock with close bolts meant to keep you off the ledge.

FA: Ben Chriswell, Chris Williams 2018

Climbers on the crux of Slab Trek's final pitch. (Courtesy John Borland / morffed.com)

UPPER WEBFOOT PROSPECT

	CRAG	SUN & HIKE	ROUTES	RANGE	PAGE
1	PBR Wall	45min	6	5.7-5.11a	58
2	The Guardian	AM 60min	5	5.10a-5.10c	62
3	Lost Wall	AM 70min	10	5.8+-5.12a	66
4	Aurora Slab	PM 65min	3	5.8-5.10c/d	69
5	Yellow Brick Road	AM 65min	1	5.8+	71

The Upper Webfoot Prospect area is seldom visited by more than the core group of climbers that visit Hatcher Pass, which is a shame, because there are some high quality routes in an excellent area. That high praise doesn't even account for the many first ascents awaiting the bold or the climbs that have been done in the past but didn't make it into this book. The best way to access this area is to park at the American Alpine Club outhouse and walk toward Toto Buttress. After crossing the river, follow the trails left toward The White Spot. Walk left around the base of The White Spot and continue heading up valley on a faint trail toward these walls. You'll pass open green areas with boulders and old mining equipment, such as the generator that looks like it's ready to be put back into use. Don't stop too early, however, there is climbing to be had!

PBR Wall 45min

Approach:
The same approach as for The White Spot, but you continue around the corner. From the outhouse, follow the trail toward the river. There are several crossing options. Once across the river, look for a trail that heads left before the Prism Boulder (the large slanted boulder on the trail). This trail will lead down into a nice meadow and then up the other side of the hill. Try and follow the trail here as it crosses through the boulders and on to a grass ramp. Continue along the trail as it heads toward the cliff. Cross underneath the left edge of the cliff and around the left corner toward the upper walls such as Lost Wall. The PBR Wall is right on the trail and hard to miss.

Area:
The PBR wall has likely seen a few ascents over the years but was only recently developed through cleaning and the installation of anchors. It is a good section of rock that you would pass on your way to the Lost Wall or Aurora Slab and is now a great place to spend the day if you don't feel like going to those further crags. The approach isn't too bad and the routes are quality.

Editor extraordinaire Lisa Delaney and Morriganne heading out to the crag before Morriganne headed off to chase the forever tail.

1 Honky Tonks & Pretty Women 5.7 ☆☆ 36m
Gear to 3", 2 bolt rap anchor
Far left of the crag and slightly around the corner. Climb blocks and ledges in the corner with most of the gear between .25" and .75". Move right after the corner onto the face with thin nut placements. Continue on ledges and blocks until you find the anchor.
FA: Chris Williams, Lang Van Dommelen 2017

2 Cheap Bourbon Whisky 5.8 ☆☆☆ 35m
3 bolts, 1 piton, Gear to 2", 2 bolt rap anchor
Climb up through the corner to the left of the roof. Move right immediately after for an airy traverse to the first bolt. Continue meandering around a bit from here following bolts with gear mixed between until the final crack before the anchor.
FA: Chris Williams, Lang Van Dommelen 2017

3 12 Pack and a Prayer 5.10b, 5.10d, 5.6 ☆☆☆☆ 75m
Pitch 1: 5.10b, 6 bolts, 1 piton, Gear to 2", 2 bolt rap anchor ☆☆☆☆ *35m*
The first pitch is the money pitch. Climb the left angling crack. Carefully traverse the detached flake and marvel at its ability to hold. Exit the crack using a piton. Extend the piton with a sling if you're going to use it or else it could cause bad drag. More fun climbing on bolts lead to the anchor.
Pitch 2: 5.10d, 8 bolts, Gear to 3", 2 bolt rap anchor ☆☆☆ *31m*
An odd meandering pitch with plenty of loose rock if you get off route. Move right after the second bolt to the first roof. Puzzle your way over by avoiding the blocks and ledge to your left. An awkward squeeze lead to an enjoyable but pumpy finish.
Pitch 3: 5.6, Gear to 2", 2 bolt anchor ☆ *9m*
This isn't so much a pitch as just top access. Dirty climbing above the anchor will get you to an anchor at the top but its not really worth it. Best to finish with Pitch 2. Rappel the route.
FA: Chris Williams, Shannon Reid, Lang Van Dommelen

The PBR Wall sits at the junction between the Upper Webfoot Prospect and Lower Webfoot Prospect areas. They span the ridge leading from The Diamond to Yellow Brick Road. At the top of the ridge is the Pinnacle. This peak has multiple routes and can be accessed from this valley, or the other side of the ridge. Many boulders also littler the upper valley, with some having some even having good landings, although only the lower areas are currently in the Alaska Bouldering Guide. Even if you don't climb in this area it is hard not to appreciate the beauty of this part of the valley. Try to remain on the trail when accessing these areas, and avoid trampling tundra where possible.

4 Morriganne's Route 5.10a, 5.10a, 5.9+ ☆☆☆☆ 72m
Pitch 1: 5.10a, 6 bolts, Gear to 1", 2 bolt rap anchor 30m
Climb chickenheads using bolts heading toward the left side of the roof above. Big holds through the roof on bolts will lead you to a flaring finger crack. May require some extra route finding on easier climbing.
Pitch 2: 5.10a, 7 bolts, Gear to 2", 2 bolt rap anchor 24m
From the belay, head straight up through the corner and follow a few more funky moves leading to the small roof above. Pull over the roof; easy climbing from here leads to the anchor.
Pitch 3: 5.9+, Gear to 3", 2 bolt rap anchor 18m
Climbing the splitter will lead to great steep climbing using the crack and face holds. Takes plenty of gear. Pull through the notch and the anchor is on the ledge above over the grass.
Descent: Do 3 rappels using a 60m rope.
FA: Chris Williams, Gus Barber, Lisa Delaney 2020

5 Surfin Turf 5.9 ☆ 30m
4 bolts, Gear to 3", 2 bolt rap anchor
Starts in a shallow corner with nubs to a chickenhead slab. Go through a roof then left into the black corner before going right to the anchor. Needs cleaning.
FA: Chris Williams 2020

6 8 Seconds to Glory 5.10a, 5.11a, 5.8 ☆☆☆ 73m
Pitch 1 - The Bucking Chute: 5.10a, 4 bolts, Gear to 4", 2 bolt rap anchor 33m
Start in a shallow, shattered crack and head up to a funky bulge, past a bolt. From the bulge gain a vegetated ledge below a double roof and corner system. Climb through two roofs. A #4 is nice here. Head up the golden corner to a bolt and exit right onto chill face climbing and a couple more bolts. Wiggle onto the sloping ledge for a 2 bolt belay.
Pitch 2 - 8 Second Ride: 5.11a, 5 bolts, Gear to .75", 2 bolt rap anchor 20m
The money pitch! Traverse left from the anchor past 3 bolts. Pull around the arete and bulge to some steep face fun and another bolt. Follow the face into a tips crack. Classic thin crack climbing to finish right on "thank Jesus" hand jams. Belay on the turf ledge.
Pitch 3 - GLORY!: 5.8, 2 bolts, Gear to 3", 2 bolt rap anchor 20m
A climb to the podium on hand jams and chicken heads. 2 bolts lead to mellow jug hauling and jamming to the top of the pillar. Cross the grass 30ft to belay.
FA: Chris Williams, Ben Chriswell 2020

1
2
3

4
5
6

The Guardian AM 60min

Approach:
Located near the Lost Wall and Yellow Brick Road so make sure to reserve enough time for the hike in and out. Start on the trail near the American Alpine Club's (AAC) outhouse and cross the river at the boulder crossing. Instead of moving right toward Zulu Wall, walk toward The White Spot. Move left of The White Spot passing the Catch the Wave gully. Continue along the base of the cliff on a somewhat defined trail and past the mining equipment including a generator. Soon after a steep uphill, this rock face looms ahead. Take a left for Yellow Brick Road or head direct for The Guardian.

Area:
There is morning sun and, although there is some overhang, it does not keep the rain off the bottom of the cliff. Solid rock on the routes with definite room for more climbs. *God's Country (5.9, 5.10b)* is the classic here; it was the first route on the wall.

God's Country (5.10b) is a route which many people feel is worth the 60 minute walk. It is a slog to this area, and the wall is not dry in the rain like the Lost Wall, but it does have some more moderate climbing. That being said, these are older climbs and I've heard many say they are sandbagged.

1 Unknown 5.10a ☆☆
2 bolts, Gear to 3", Sling anchor
Currently I don't know much about this route. I have heard it goes at 5.10a although I have not climbed it. I am including it for reference only. Start with 2 bolts on slabs and then go to natural gear. Climb direct until you find a large boulder to sling or hidden anchors.
FA: Steve Garvey

2 God's Country 5.10a, 5.10b ☆☆☆☆☆ 55m
Pitch 1: 5.10a, 2 bolts, Gear to 3", 2 bolt anchor ☆☆☆☆☆ 40m
Start in the cave section of the detached boulder and move left into a crack system. Continue left along a ramp then right toward the first large roof. Move along very well protected climbing into the roof crux. There are two bolts here for an older anchor or continue up and right of the next large roof for a more comfortable belay. Bring lots of slings. Double rope rappel.
Pitch 2: 5.10b, Gear to 3", Slings anchor ☆ 15m
The second pitch is shorter than the first and includes some blocky climbing through several roofs. Find blocks to anchor to and double rope rappel. This pitch is not listed on the picture below as I am not sure where it heads.
FA: Jim Sweeney, Shawn Toohey, Paul Wharton

3 God's Country Var. 5.10 ☆☆☆ 40m
6 bolts, Gear to 3", 2 bolt anchor
Start just right of the detached boulder cave and move right two bolts. Move left at the third and continue left along flakes to a corner. Climb the corner direct to the roof meeting with and finishing on *Gods Country*.

4 Pastures of Heaven 5.10c ☆☆☆ 25m
11 bolts, 2 bolt anchor
Begins just right of the detached boulder and is the same start as *Gods Country Var.* Move right on bolts and face moves to the arete meeting with *Pearly Gates*. Continue the arete to the anchors. Gear helps to eliminate runouts.
FA: Steve Garvey, Jim Sweeney

5 Pearly Gates 5.10c ☆☆☆ 25m
9 bolts, 2 bolt anchor
Start high on the grass ramp at a triple corner system. Climb on bolts moving right to the arete. Follow the arete to the anchor. Gear can help on these routes to eliminate runouts.
FA: Steve Garvey, Jim Sweeney

Jim Schloemer high on Terrorvision at the Lost Wall. Terrorvision is a classic of Hatcher Pass and a testpiece for many. (Courtesy Caleb Helkenn)

Lost Wall AM 70min

Approach:

Park near the American Alpine Club outhouse and walk the well-worn trail down toward the river. Cross the river on boulders and begin the trek left toward The White Spot. Walk left around the wall and continue left until in the large boulder field. Do not take any of the side offshoot valleys which lead up the hill. Walk up the grass valley staying on the lower edge of the vertical sections on the right. Staying on the grass and off the boulders will save time. Pass mining equipment, which includes a large generator, and continue up the valley staying close to the mountain side. Scramble a short steep section, and it will bring you to The Guardian. Walk up right of the wall to what looks like it will be a drop off. You should be able to see the wall from here on your left. Move left across the grass and curve right, side hilling to the base of the rock face.

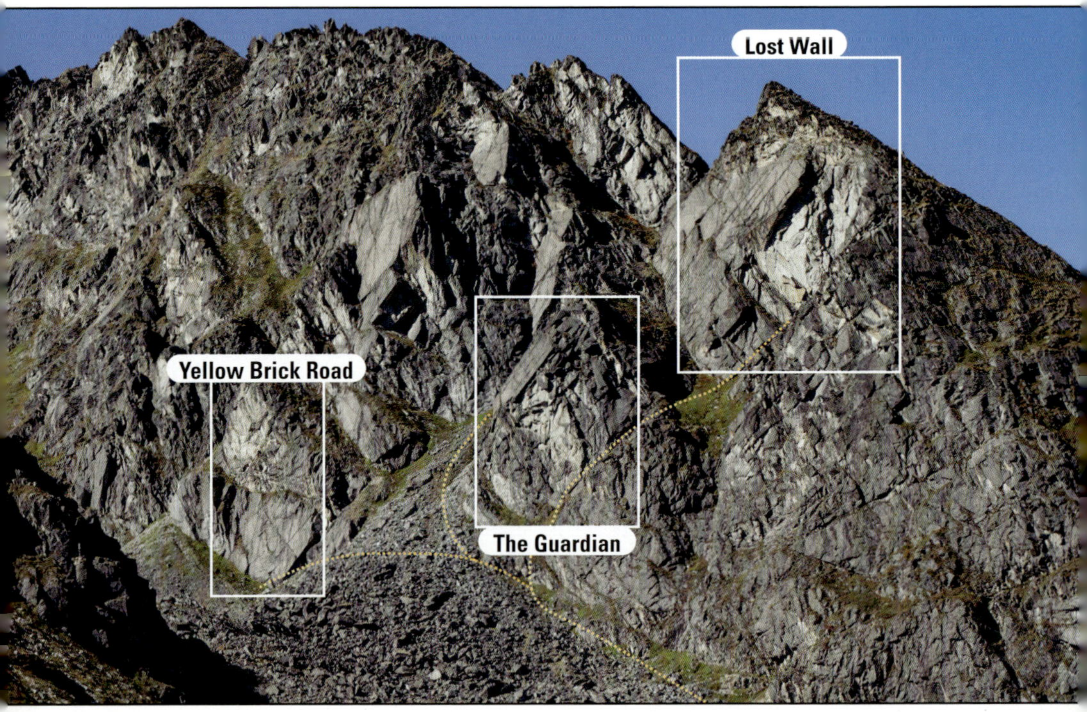

Area:

The wall is overhanging and is dry in the rain. Watch the raindrops fall 20 feet away from you as you belay near the base of the cliff. That also means that the routes are steep and most often difficult. There is something eerie about this area making it even more of an adventure than it already is. Many people I have talked to called this wall "intimidating." Doesn't get much sun but the bonus is that the wall stays dry. The best sun can be during the mid-afternoon depending on the time of the season.

Several routes saw a few changes over the last few years. *Rainman (5.11)* was finished to the top of the wall and *Pheonix (5.12a)* got a clean ascent, as it was previously listed as a partial aid route.

1 No Name 5.11

2 bolts, 1 piton + 1 wire anchor

Start just left of the main ramp on a steep face. Climb two bolts with chain hangers to a slabby ledge and end before the next ramp.

FA: Paul Turecki

2 Original Route 5.10a ☆☆☆

3 pitches, Trad rack

The original route on the Lost Wall. Follow the ramp up left and around the corner before hooking right to an anchor. Continue direct along the face with odd angled cracks to the top before the rock turns white again. Bring your trad rack.

FA: Steve Garvey, Jim Sweeney

William Zachares climbing Terrorvision under the main roof of the Lost Wall. (Courtesy Brian Prince)

3 Terrorvision 5.6, 5.12a ☆☆☆☆☆ 55m

Pitch 1: 5.6, Gear to 1", 2 bolt anchor 35m

Climb the easy 5.6 ramp on the left side of the crag to a 2 bolt anchor below the crack start of *Terrorvision.*

Pitch 2: 5.12a, 7 bolts, 4 pitons, Gear to 3", 2 bolt rap anchor 20m

Move into the immediate shattered crack going up to the roof and bring your reserves. Move right along the large roof until it ends. This route is often considered to be sandbagged. Double rope rappel mandatory. Epic.

FA: Steve Garvey, Jay Rowe

4 Shake and Bake 5.10a, 5.11a A1 ☆☆☆

Pitch 1: 5.10a, Gear to 3", 2 bolt anchor

Take the obvious cracks on the right side and move left to the anchors which are on the top of a large detached flake, this pitch is off-width (5.10a).

Var. 2: Move across the easy 5.6 slab and climb right on a very wide crack to the anchors. (5.7)

Pitch 2: 5.11a A1, 5 bolts, 5 pitons, Gear to 3", 2 bolt anchor

Climb at a 45 degree angle left until the crack meets with *Terrorvision* early in the roof. The bolts and most of the pins are found on the *Terrorvision* portion. The crack has yet to see a free ascent and guesses are at 5.12 if you are feeling ambitious. Double rope rappel.

FA: Jim Sweeney, Pat Rinehart

5 Phoenix 5.12a ☆☆☆ 21m

9+ bolts, Gear to .5", 2 bolt anchor

Climb following bolts on clean rock until it meets with *Rainman* for a few moves. Then go left on a crack for gear and bolts. This route was 5.10 A1 until recently freed.

FFA: Ben Chriswell

FA: Jason Moncrieff, Pat Rinehart 09.10.2010

6 Rainman 5.10d, 5.11 ☆☆☆☆ 40m

Pitch 1: 5.10d, Gear to 3", 2 bolt anchor

Same start as *Ironman* on the large block. Move immediately left at the ramp onto the face and another crack to the flake. Follow the thin finger crack and traverse right out of the small roof. Shares anchors with *Ironman.*

Pitch 2: 5.11, Bolts, 1 piton, 2 bolt rap anchor

Recently unfinished until climbed by Ben Chriswell and Brock Rust. There were additional bolts added as well. Go up a steep corner directly above the belay, gear will help to fill in between bolts. Go left after the corner to a horizontal where a BD #3 is good. Go to the *Terrorvision* anchor.

FA P1: Jim Sweeney

FA P2: Ben Chriswell & Brock Rust

7 Ironman 5.10b, 5.11b/c ☆☆☆ 45m

Pitch 1: 5.10b, 1 piton, Gear to 2", 2 bolt anchor

Start in a complex corner and climb continuing along in the corner until pulling out left onto a ramp, which is the crux. Move left along the ramp until the anchor.

Pitch 2: 5.11b/c, 3 bolts, 5 pitons, Gear to 2", 2 bolt anchor

Move immediately left of the anchors to an undercling ramp. Climb to the first bolt and go direct on bolts and pins through a crack. Trends left on easier ground and meets with *Terrorvision* before moving out right to the anchors. May use a few pins of *Terrorvision* once meeting with the route. Double rope rappel is mandatory once committing to the second pitch.

FA: Jim Sweeney, Steve Garvey

8 Rineman 5.10c ☆☆

5 bolts, 1 piton, Gear to .5", 2 bolt anchor

Start most of the way up the hill on a ramp that leans left and is wide enough for good feet. Gear and one piton to the first bolt. From the face move left into a corner, going too far into the corner is slightly off route, although doable. Move right at the anchor.

FA: Pat Rinehart, Clifford Hilpert

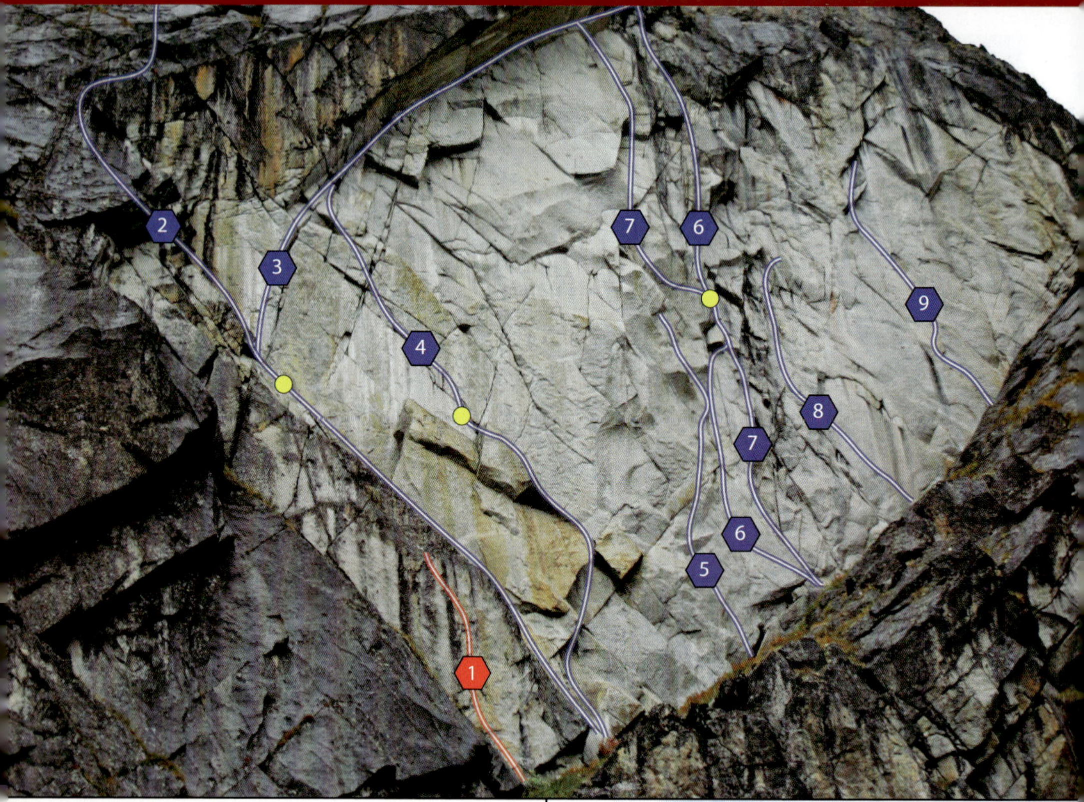

9 Unknown 5.10c ☆☆
8 bolts, Gear to 3", 1 bolt + 1 piton anchor
Begin high uphill before the grass ramp ends. An obvious large flake which trends left before hooking right under a roof for the anchors. The bolts currently do not have hangers. There is a runout between the last bolt and the anchor where protection is necessary.
FA: Paul Turecki

10 Persistance 5.8+, 5.8+ ☆☆☆ **45m**
Pitch 1: 5.8+, Gear to 1", 2 bolt anchor, 1 bolt belay anchor
This route climbs the corner on the right side of the ramp that goes up the front of the Lost Wall. Traverse right along the ledge passing a large suspended block to a belay bolt with gear available as a backup. Follow through the corner for the first anchor before a right angling crack.
Pitch 2: 5.8+, Gear to 3", 1 bolt + Gear anchor
Follow the right crack and then a left angling crack to get on top of the formation. There is a bolt at the top for the anchor. From the anchor above you can rappel back into the gully for the Lost Wall with a single 60m rope.
FA: Steve Garvey, Jim Sweeney

Aurora Slab PM 65min

Approach:
Located behind The Guardian so make sure to reserve enough time for the hike in and out. Start on the trail near the American Alpine Club's (AAC) outhouse and cross the river at the boulder crossing. Instead of moving right toward Zulu Wall, walk toward The White Spot. Move left of The White Spot passing the Catch the Wave gully. Continue along the base of the cliff on a somewhat defined trail and past the mining equipment including a generator. Soon after a steep uphill, the face of The Guardian will be directly ahead. The Aurora Slab is the backside of The Guardian formation. Walk around left of the formation and hook right up the gully until you see the Aurora Slab on your right. Don't count on any definitive trail for most of this hike. Just stay high on the grass and out of the gullies unless you're sure that is the one you are supposed to go into.

Area:
The original route was put up by Steve Garvey and Jim Sweeney. Most of the routes in this area seem to have at least one of these names in it. A new two bolt anchor was finally added to the top of this area and makes the rappel more enjoyable. This is an excellent place to practice your slab technique as it is a good long climb with many stopper placements.

A picture of the old knot and tat that served as the anchor above these climbs for decades. With permission from the first ascenionist a new two bolt anchor was finally added on top.
(Courtesy John Borland / morffed.com)

1 Aurora Slabialous 5.8 ☆☆☆☆☆ 40m

Gear to .5", 2 bolt rap anchor

Bring your stoppers as they are very handy here. Climb the extremely obvious dihedral. The climbing can range from wet to loads of enjoyment depending on the day. Double rope rappel.

FA: Jim Sweeney, Steve Garvey, 1987

2 Zero Tolerance 5.10c/d ☆☆☆ 40m

Gear to 1", 2 bolt rap anchor

Four meters to the right of *Aurora Slabialous*, this route climbs thin cracks through the center of the face. It often fills with moss but when clean can be an excellent route. Stoppers are great for this route as well as small cams or Camp Ball Nuts.

FA: Jim Sweeney, Dave Nyman 1989

It took thirty years for this wall to finally get a new anchor. The previous sling and stopper in a crack was less than inspiring even if it kept the old-school Hatcher feel. Fear not, you'll probably find plenty of sketchy anchors exploring these areas.

3 Speakin' to Allah 5.10a/r ☆☆ 38m

Gear to .25", 2 bolt rap anchor

This route follows intermittent cracks in an arch away from the previous route and ends at the same place. It is a runout even with the best gear, will probably need to be cleaned up so bring a nut tool to make placements. Bring Lowe or Camp Ball Nuts.

FA: Jim Sweeney, Steve Garvey, 1989

Yosemite Decimal System

Initially referred to as the Tahquitz Decimal System, it was based on 10 climbs on Tahquitz Rock in Idyllwild, California, with the most difficult being Open Book at 5.9. This climb was considered the most difficult in the country in 1952. Climbing has come a long way, we now have ratings as high as 5.15d, and the ratings continue to get tested. The letters were added to the number rating in the 1960's.

(Courtesy John Borland / morffed.com)

Yellow Brick Road AM 65min

Approach:
Park near the American Alpine Club's (AAC) outhouse and walk the well-worn trail to the river. Cross the river on boulders and begin the trek left toward The White Spot. Walk left around the wall and continue left until in the large boulder field. Do not take any of the side right offshoot valleys which lead up the hill. Walk up the grass valley staying on the lower edge of the vertical sections on the right. Staying on the grass and off the boulders will save time. Pass mining equipment which includes a large generator and continue up the valley staying close to the mountain side. Scramble a short steep section, and it will bring you to The Guardian. Walk left crossing a small boulder field, and it will drop down into the Yellow Brick Road area. The wall will be on your right.

Area:
This is another one of the walls located in a great concentration of rock with anchors and routes strewn throughout this giant area. There are many routes in this area that are not in this book, including several Chris Williams routes at this crag. There is an over-abundance of rock surrounding this cliff and many possibilities for new routes. Hopefully the other routes in the area will find their way into this book; until then expect to explore and find hidden treasures all through the valley.

1 Yellow Brick Road 5.8+ ☆☆☆☆ 37m
9 bolts, Gear to 1.5", 2 bolt rap anchor
Start low on the wall just left of the overhangs and climb to the giant X of cracks in the wall. Then aim direct and over a small roof. Double rope rappel. There is a second pitch. I hear it could use a few bolts and an anchor since currently it is a gear anchor or walkoff from the top of the second pitch.
FA: Steve Garvey, David Whitelaw

(Courtesy William Finley)

FAIRANGEL VALLEY WALLS

	CRAG	SUN & HIKE	ROUTES	RANGE	PAGE
1	3rd Generation	AM 40min	3	5.10a-5.12	74
2	Veinous Wall	AM 40min	4	5.8-5.10a	76
3	Wishbone Wall	25min	14	5.7-5.12d	79
4	Tunnel Vision	PM 30min	11	5.7-5.11d	85
5	Tin Can Rock	PM 35min	4	5.7-5.11c/d	88
6	BPR Wall	PM 70min	4	5.8-5.11b/r	90

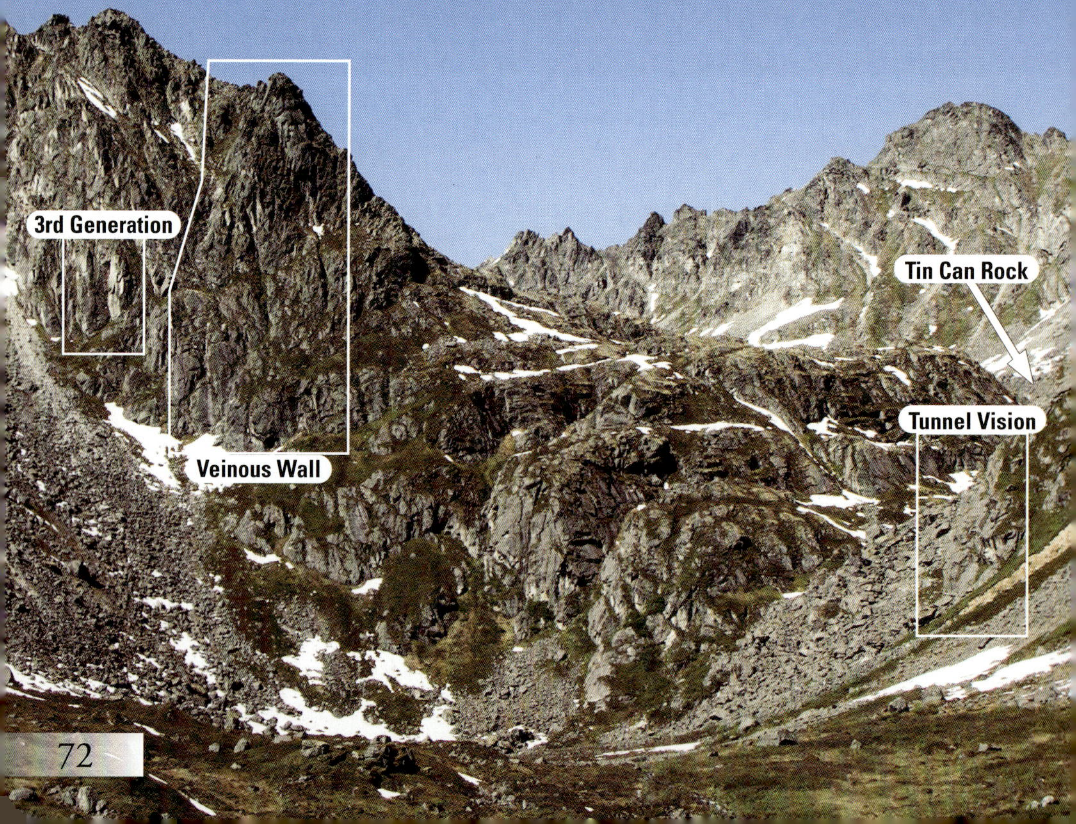

The Fairangel Valley is a treasure trove of great routes with a quick approach and an abundance of sun. This small area of the valley has plenty of fun moderates for the new climber or hard routes for the advanced. It is also one of the best places to go for a swim, with several beautiful lakes that have small schools of fish that somehow make it through the winter. The best way to access this valley is to park at the end of Archangel Road and walk back downhill about 60m, looking for a trail that heads down toward the river. This trail should head along the right side of the creek toward the gap in the valley. At any point, you can break off and head toward the crag you want to go to, with the exception of the BPR Wall. You'll want to go through Fairangel Gap and past Tin Can Rock before going up the mountainside toward the crag.

3rd Generation AM 40min

Approach:
To approach, park near the end of Archangel Road and take a trail left before the gate. There are several, and most should lead in the same direction toward Fairangel Valley. Hike toward the lakes, and stay on the right side of the lower valley river. When at the boulder field, which leads up Fairangel Gap, stay below the gap and move left along the mountainside. You'll pass below the lower section of Tunnel Vision and cross just above Fairangel Lakes. Head up the mountainside, staying primarily on the grass/moss sections as the rocks can be very loose on the talus sections. This wall is above the Veinous Wall and you won't get a good look at it until right underneath the wall.

Area:
This crag feels like it is in a state of development, although not much has been done to it in the last few years. Despite the lack of anchors on some routes and a clear direction on others, this is still an enjoyable wall with *3rd Generation* being the obvious gem of the crag. It is an excellent route that starts hard and doesn't let up much before the anchor.

1 More Playin, Less Sprayin 5.11a ☆☆☆ 10m
5 bolts, Gear to .5", 1 bolt anchor
This route climbs the dike features on the left side of the wall. There are a few places for gear to eliminate runouts. The anchor, as of this writing, was a single bolt without a hanger. Instead it had a slung nut with a quicklink.
FA: Dan Kryger, Andy Hoyt

2 3rd Generation 5.11d, 5.12 ☆☆☆☆ 25m
Pitch 1: 5.11d, 6 bolts, Gear to .75", 2 bolt anchor
This climb has a hard start and doesn't let up much. It should test your endurance as you head toward the roof and one more crux before the anchor.
Pitch 2: 5.12, 3 bolts, Gear to 3", 2 bolt anchor
This pitch has the crux at the first 3 bolts from the anchor and then continues on gear to the top of the cliff.
FA: Dan Kryger, Andy Hoyt
FFA: Aaron Thrasher

3 Redhead Arete 5.10a ☆ 25m
3 bolts, Gear to 3", Gear anchor
This route climbs the right arete 8m from *Third Generation*. The route climbs through large blocks, broken cracks, and awkward placements. It probably ends at the top of the cliff somewhere, although I'm not sure where. Be prepared to leave gear for an anchor. Bring lots of gear of all sizes.
FA: Andy Hoyt, Greg Matthews

3rd Generation is an excellent climb with fun moves and even a roof to pull. The rest of the climbs in this area feel somewhat more adventurous as they may be missing hangers or have a more wandering nature.

Willie Dalton on Pitch 4 of Toto (pg. 39) with Jacob VanHoomissen belaying. (Courtesy Wongi Kim)

Veinous Wall AM 40min

Approach:
To approach, park near the end of Archangel Road and take a trail left before the gate. There are several trails, and most should lead in the same direction toward Fairangel Valley. Hike toward the lakes and stay on the right side of them. When at the boulder field, which leads up Fairangel Gap, stay below the gap and move left along the mountainside. There are a few walls which look like they could take some fun routes. Veinous Wall is located 10 minutes uphill from the lakes.

Area:
It may seem weird to include this wall when there is a ton of rock in the area, and this is just one little wall. Some of these areas I have included just to get others out, and putting up new routes while exploring the few that are already there. The wall has seen a lot of cleaning especially on *The Girlfriend Route*, which is now an excellent clean line. *Rainbow Country* requires a keen sense of route finding and will end on the top of the tower above the Veinous Wall, which is also known as the Warmup Wall.

1 Original Route 5.8 ☆☆ 32m
Gear to 2", 2 bolt anchor
The same start as the other routes but head left on blocky terrain. Follow thin cracks avoiding the dirt or grass. Move right at the finish, and use the same anchor as *The Girlfriend Route*.
FA: Andy Hoyt, Dan Kryger

2 The Girlfriend Route 5.10a ☆☆☆☆ 32m
4 bolts, 1 piton, Gear to .75", 2 bolt anchor
Start on a blocky section of rock up easy ground to a ledge. Walk right along the ledge to a crack that angles right below the bolts. Follow the crack high on gear and clip the first bolt. Follow bolts with gear in the middle before the piton and the anchor high over the lip. Excellent route.
FA: Andy Hoyt, Greg Matthews

3 Rainbow Country aka Warmup Tower 5.10a (6 pitches) ☆☆☆ 420m
This route of up to 6 pitches starts on *The Girlfriend Route* and continues up and right on 4th class toward the headwall of the upper tower. On the upper tower, start with a hanging traverse to a heel hook and follow cracks of varying sizes to the top of the tower. Bring gear to 3". All gear anchors after first pitch. The route will also be in the shade for most of the day so bring adequate clothing. Walkoff through Fairangel Valley.
FA: Andy Hoyt, Amos Swanson

4 Clogged Aorta 5.8 ☆☆ 33m
Gear to 2", 2 bolt anchor
Climb on top of the right block with a ledge and into the obvious large right leaning crack. Follow the crack right and head up through a dirty grassy section. Getting better but it still needs more cleaning.
FA: Kelsey Gray, John Borland

3
2
4
1

Elaina Julayha climbing the first pitch of Toto (p.37). (Courtesy John Borland)

Wishbone Wall 25min

Approach:
The Wishbone Wall is one of the most obvious walls toward Fairangel Valley due to its proximity to the ridge line and the parking area. From the end of Archangel Road, park close to the gate. Look for a trail on the left hand side that is about 50m from the gate. This trail leads to Fairangel Valley. Continue on the trail staying on the right side of the lower river until you are in line with the wall. Continue up grass ramps to the base.

Area:
Wishbone Wall has become one of my favorite crags during the summer for casual climbing due to its proximity to the road, rebolted climbs, and casual atmosphere. This wall sat for years with little to no attention. It would randomly get a party of climbers that came by only to leave frustrated at the lack of quality routes or good hardware. In reality there were plenty of good routes at the wall, they just needed a little work. After several years of rebolting and some development, this wall should once again see plenty of climbing. The last few years saw much of the cliff cleaned up and most of the leftover older bolts were removed and replaced. Several new routes such as *Because Science (5.10a)* and *The Rain Game (5.8)* help fill in the gaps making, this area an excellent place to spend an entire day cragging. It is usually one of the last areas for sun, which can make it feel like a bit of an oven during the middle of summer but is perfect during the colder days or to get that golden tan.

cience 5.10a ☆☆☆☆ **28m**
o anchor
d line at the crag. Climb through
broken rock to a clean face. Excellent moves lead up to an exciting finish before the anchor. An enjoyable addition to the crag.
FA: Kelsey Gray, Ryan Senko 2018

2 Unknown 5.10a ☆☆☆☆ **33m**
2 bolts, Gear to 2", 2 bolt rap anchor
Fun steep climbing on good holds. Start on the white rock and climb to one bolt. Follow slightly right for the rest of the climb toward a steep upper face with one more bolt before the anchor. Exciting face moves for the upper crux. There is room for a possible BD#4 but can be avoided with a slight runout.

3 Unknown 5.10a ☆☆☆ **33m**
3 bolts, Gear to 2", 2 bolt rap anchor
Climb 3 meters right of the previous bolted face and big holds on a steep rounded arete. Meet with the previous climb by going left after the bolts and under the roof. Climb toward the high upper bolt on the face.

4 Stan Deazy 5.9+ ☆☆☆☆ **20m**
2 bolts, Gear to 3", 2 bolt rap anchor
Start low on the slab and climb to the crack that has excellent stances for each placement. From the top of the crack move right onto the slab for two bolts before the anchor above the next climb.
FA: Kelsey Gray, Sterling Anderson 2016

5 The Rain Game 5.8 ☆☆☆ **17m**
5 bolts, Gear to 1", 2 bolt rap anchor
A .75 and #1 BD works as well as possible micro stoppers before the first bolt, although most will find them unnecessary. Continue over the nice big holds to the arete. The second bolt helps keep the rope off of the sharp block at the lip, it is a good idea to keep it as a directional when toproping. Stays mostly right of the bolts at the arete. Same anchor as *Stan Deazy*.
FA: Rachel Lowrance, Kelsey Gray

6 Wishbone Left 5.10a ☆☆ **15m**
1 bolt, Gear to 1", 2 bolt rap anchor
A short pitch in a corner that splits in a Y. Climb the left face on gear with a big gap between the ground and the first piece. Mostly small gear. It is possible to exit the top early and skip the final crux move through the upper lip by going left on the arete.
FA: Paul Turecki, Mugs Stump

Shasta Gray belays Dan Linnell as he nears the anchor of Unknown #9 with only the 2 bolts clipped in. This climb can often feel pretty airy.

7 Last Dry Place in the Universe 5.11b/r ☆☆☆ 17m
2 bolts, Gear to .25", 2 bolt rap anchor
Climbs out right of a double roof and starts the same as the previous route. Some gear trickery may be possible in the middle between the bolts, but I wouldn't count on it. I am not sure about the leadability of this route, it is better toproped from the *Broken Head* anchor.. The anchor is just to the right of the roof.
FA: Paul Turecki, Mugs Stump

8 Broken Head 5.12d ☆☆☆ 15m
6 bolts, 2 bolt rap anchor
This route starts on steep sidepulls and gets hard fast. Climb the steep arete on sharp thin holds to an anchor just right of the roof. The crux is between the second and third bolt. The rest of the route, while easier, still manages to pack its own punch.
FA: Paul Turecki

9 Unknown 5.10b PG13 ☆☆☆ 30m
2 bolts, Gear to 4", 2 bolt rap anchor
Scramble the grass ledge below the featured face with a sharp arete. Start on the left and climb past the bolt. Traverse a thin foot ledge right around the arete to a bolt on the other side. Continue on gear along the left face to the anchor, which is high on the cliff.

10 Sacktapped by a GriGri 5.10a ☆☆☆☆ 18m
3 bolts, Gear to 1", 3 bolt rap anchor
Fun varied climbing up the clean face. Climb a short thin crack toward the great undercling. Go straight up the bolts and through the small roof above. Once over the top, walk right up the ramp to use the same anchor as *In Record Time*. There is a bolt on the top ramp that is best to leave in as a directional to eliminate a large swing for the follower.
FA: Kelsey Gray, Sterling Anderson 2016

11 In Record Time 5.8 ☆☆☆½ 15m
5 bolts, 3 bolt rap anchor
This fun short sport line takes some thinking. Start low on easy ground and climb to the first ledge with a bolt. Head along the corner to the anchor above the lip.
FA: Kelsey Gray, Sterling Anderson 2016

12 Blades of Glory 5.10a ☆☆☆ 17m
5 bolts, 2 bolt rap anchor
This route starts on a ledge that is 7 meters left of the anchor for *In Record Time*. The best way to get to the anchor is to climb one of the previous two routes, then from the anchor, walk roped along the ledge toward a small grass area where there is a 2 bolt belay anchor. From the anchor, head right along the ramp making interesting moves to the face above. Follow the arete on bolts to the anchor on the top of the formation. For the follower, it is best to stay clipped into the third bolt until after you've pulled the crux lip move to the ledge. The leader can be lowered back to the anchor for *In Record Time* where it is easier to belay the follower.
FA: Kelsey Gray, Sterling Anderson 2016

13 Unknown 5.12a/r ☆☆☆ 9m
3 bolts, 2 bolt anchor
Thin moves on orange rock with ground fall potential at the last bolt. Sound fun? Then climb this. A short climb up the left of the short cliff. Clipping the third bolt is exciting. Easy to setup as a toprope.

14 Don't Throw Rocks 5.7 ☆☆ 9m
Toprope, 1 bolt, 2 bolt anchor
This short route can be fun for a beginner climb. The bolt on the top is for a directional. It is better to use the 2 bolt anchor that is for the previous climb. Follow the easiest path up the short face.

The 2018 UAA Rock Climbing Class enjoying the sun on the right side of the Wishbone Wall.

1
2
3
4
5
6
7
8
9

12
11
10
13
14

the hoarding marmot

Alaska's Technical Outdoor Gear Consignment Store

907-334-3333 Open 7 Days a Week

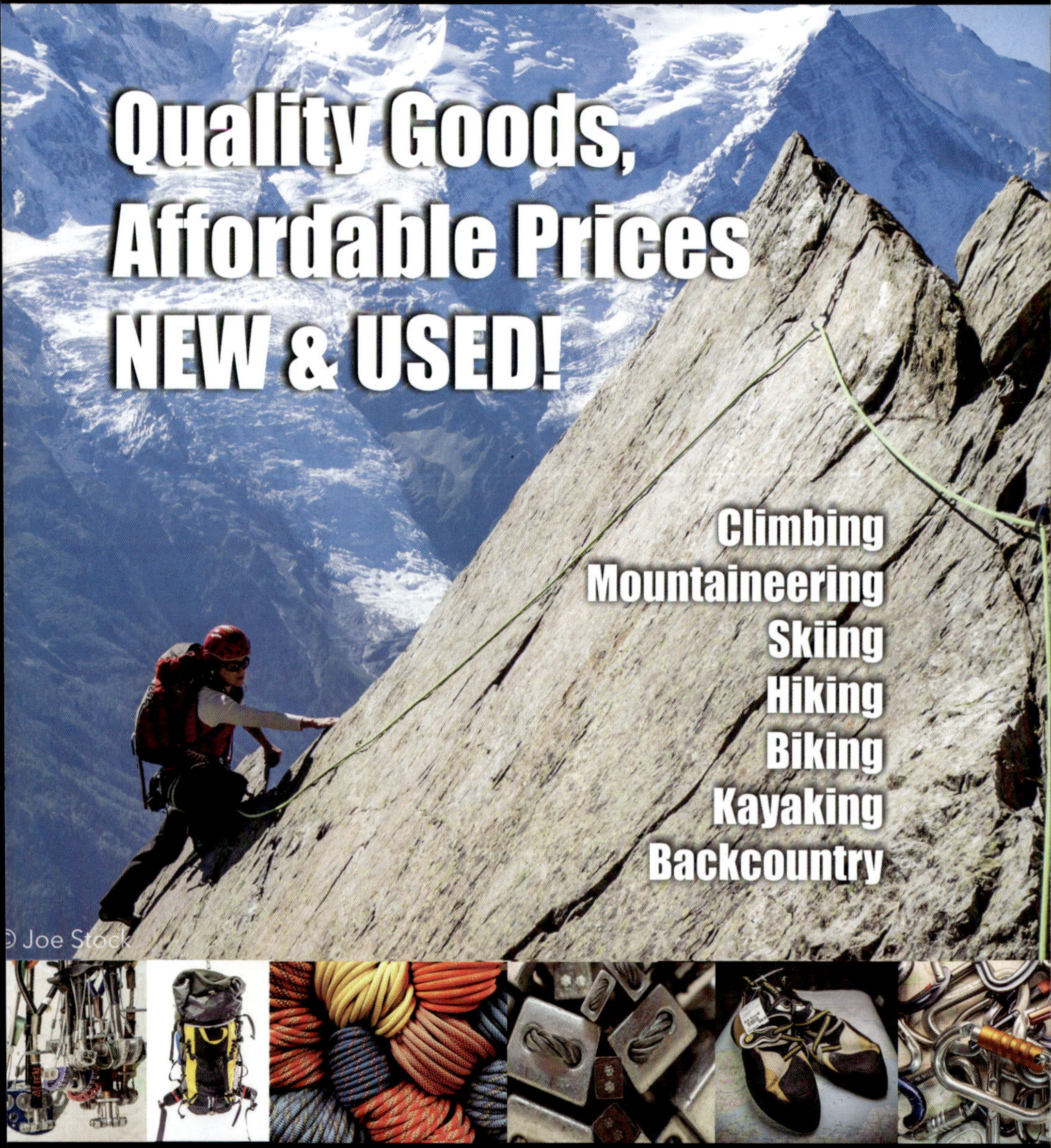

1231 W Northern Lights Blvd
Anchorage, AK 99503

info@hoardingmarmot.com
www.hoardingmarmot.com

Tunnel Vision PM 30min

Approach:

The approach for Tunnel Vision is the same as BPR Wall only you stop a lot sooner. From the American Alpine Club's (AAC) outhouse the trail will be about halfway to the gate at the end. There are many trails that go to the left; try and find the most worn trail and follow as it heads toward Fairangel Lakes and Gap. Follow the trail, staying on the right of the lakes and head directly toward Fairangel Gap. The crag will be on your right.

Area:

A climb so good it gets its own area. The main gem is *Tunnel Vision (5.11d)* a crack that splits the clean rock and is probably the best of its grade at such an accessible area. The older classics such as *Turecki Classic (5.11b)* have been rebolted, replacing some older buttonheads and making these climbs more accessible for those unwilling to risk their life on recalled hardware. The newer routes have had plenty of cleaning and most should be ready to see many ascents, especially *Matt's Crack (5.9)*, which has an excellent upper section that just begs to be climbed when standing below. There is only one new route in this edition from the last book, although there are several climbs above this area that are not included. These new routes were done by several different parties and are both sport and trad. Exploration above will bring you to several shorter blocks with anchors on them.

Vision 5.11d ☆☆☆☆☆ **15m**
bolt anchor
An excellent finger crack that splits a clean face. Hopefully your fingers are the right size. Bring an abundance of small to medium gear for the clean upper section. There is a crack that continues from the anchor on the top of the finger crack. It is a very easy climb and relatively insignificant.
FA: Paul Turecki, Leo Americus 1989

2 Unknown 5.7 ☆☆ **18m**
Toprope, 2 bolt anchor
Another route with plenty of loose rock. Starts on the highest grass ledge and heads toward the left angling crack. Uses the same anchor as *Birthday Bang.*

3 Birthday Bang 5.8 ☆☆ **21m**
2 bolts, Gear to 3", 2 bolt anchor
Start low on the formation and head toward a few bolts with gear between, avoiding any of the bad rock. First ascent was on Chris Williams birthday.
FA: Chris Williams, Gus Barber 2016

4 Matt's Crack 5.9 ☆☆☆☆ **40m**
Gear to 3", 2 bolt rap anchor
A dirty ledge start leads to a clean middle crack. From the top of a giant flake move left to make a few gear placements. This is the crux of the route. There is an anchor far off to the right on the large ledge that can be used but is meant for a different climb. If you do use the anchor make sure to place directionals for the follower or face a big swing. The route is intended to be climbed in one pitch. From the ledge, there is excellent climbing in a clean crack. I've heard this took 10 hours of cleaning from the first ascentionist, and it is greatly appreciated. Once over the crack, the anchor is higher then expected. Rappel back to the ledge and anchor or you can rappel directly down the face to the anchor of *Birthday Bang.* A single 70m rope just barely makes it to the ground from the upper anchor when rappelling direct.
FA: Chris Williams, Matt Cauda, Lisa Delaney

5 Pandemic Special 5.8+ ☆☆☆ **22m**
Bolts, Gear to 3", 2 bolt rap anchor
A new route that follows the face and ledges to the right of *Matt's Crack.* As this is a new route that was recently cleaned it should improve over time as it gets additional traffic. It was in development during the printing of this book and should be finished by the time it comes out.
FA: Chris Williams

6 Renegades of Funk 5.9+ ☆☆☆☆ **20m**
Gear to 1", 2 bolt rap anchor
4 meters left of *Unknown #7.* Start on big ledges with small gear to the bolted crux. Continue on gear and easier climbing to the high anchor. A fun route with a well protected crux. It helps to have stoppers.
FA: Chris Williams, Lisa Delaney

7 Unknown 5.10a ☆☆☆ **18m**
2 bolts, Gear to .75", 2 bolt rap anchor
This line is just to the left of the orange face and has two finish variations.
Var 1: Start on an indented section of rock to the left of the orange face. After the second bolt hook right to meet with *Turecki Classic* and finish on the close anchor. This was the original finish of the climb. (18m)
Var 2: Continue direct toward a high short crack and run it out until you can place in the crack. More ledge pulls lead to an anchor high on the cliff. Uses the higher of three anchors close to each other. (23m)

8 Turecki Classic 5.11b ☆☆☆☆ 20m
3 bolts, 1 bashie, Gear to 1", 2 bolt rap anchor
Just to the left of the roof on clean orange rock, this route has excellent moves on clean rock. The first piece of protection is an old copperhead jammed into place.
FA: Paul Turecki, Leo Americus 1988

9 Unknown 5.9 ☆☆☆ 24m
1 bolt, 1 piton, Gear to 1", 2 bolt rap anchor
The same start up the arete as the next route but moves left along a crack at the face and follows the long left leaning crack to the top. Uses the same anchor as *Turecki Classic*.

10 Cock Nose 5.9 ☆☆☆☆ 29m
6 bolts, Gear to 1", 2 bolt rap anchor
A fun route up clean climbing. Start on a small arete and then follow a short crack right toward the upper face. Meander along the face on thin holds to make your way to the upper anchor.
FA: Chris Williams, David Hertel

11 Titty Sprinkles 5.7+ ☆☆☆ 14m
2 bolts, Gear to 1", 2 bolt rap anchor
A solitary climb on this small section of wall. Climb to a small short crack and then bolts to the top along easy ledges. This is a great beginner climb.
FA: Chris Williams, David Hertel

Tin Can Rock PM 35min

Approach:
The approach for Tin Can Rock is the same as Tunnel Vision, only it is just above that crag. From the American Alpine Club's (AAC) outhouse, the trail will be about halfway to the gate at the end. There are many trails that go to the left; try and find the most worn trail and follow as it heads toward Fairangel Lakes and Gap. Follow staying on the right of the lakes and head directly toward Fairangel Gap. Pass by Tunnel Vision and continue along the base until you pass into Fairangel Gap. This wall sits directly in Fairangel Gap and is hard to see until you are nearly at it.

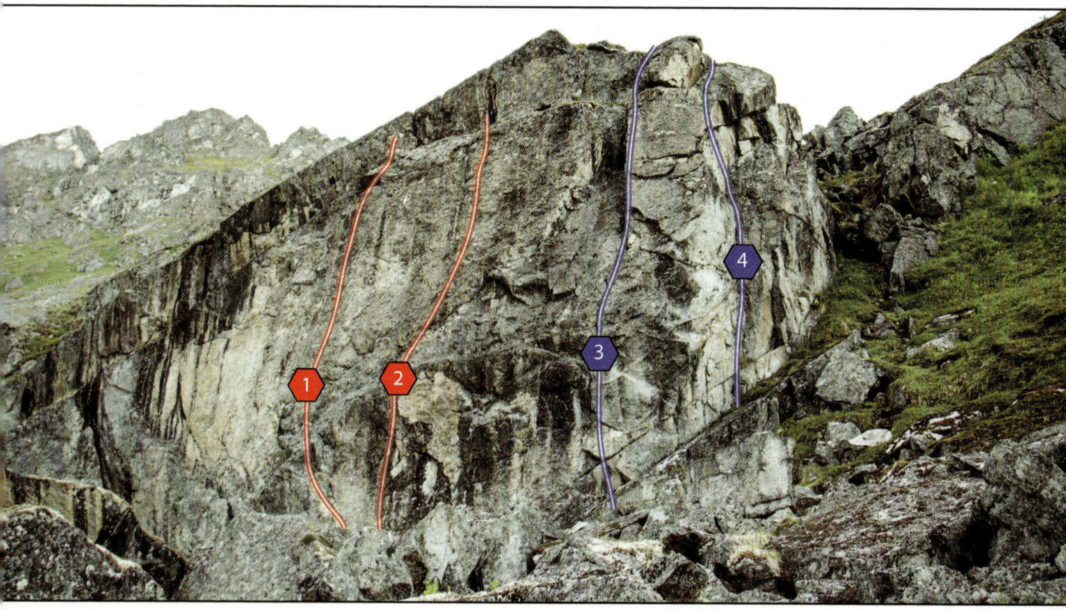

Area:
This small area has a few fun hard lines on clean steep rock with some interesting features. Plenty of crimps to be found on these routes as well as a flake that actually does look just like Africa. The routes on the right are the original lines and they are starting to clean up over time but it is still important to wear a helmet and beware of loose blocks. There is a project route to the left of *Epidemic* that still hasn't seen a first ascent. It is likely in the 5.13 range.

1 Epidemic 5.11c/d ☆☆☆ **12m**
5 bolts, 2 bolt rap anchor
Step left into immediate no-fall territory from the boulder. Puzzle your way through the hard crimpy upper face.
FA: Chris Williams, Eliza Stokes, Lang Van Dommelen 2013

2 African Dreams 5.10c ☆☆☆☆ **12m**
5 bolts, 2 bolt rap anchor
Step off the center of the larger boulder and pull a few committing moves to the first bolt. Great climbing up the steep face. Look for Africa on the wall and you'll know you're on the right route.
FA: Chris Williams, Eliza Stokes, Lang Van Dommelen 2013

3 Canned Jam 5.7 ☆☆ **15m**
Gear to 3", 2 bolt anchor
Starts with some enjoyable crack climbing and ends in dirt and some loose blocks.
FA: Bill Richards

4 Can Opener 5.7 💣 **15m**
Gear to 3.5", 2 bolt anchor
Start on a wide crack and move into a corner. Follow up and left to finish over the formation. Loose blocks and dirty.
FA: Bill Richards

Steve Garvey

Garvey was always happy to be on the ice. (Courtesy Tom Evans)

As you thumb through the pages of this guide, you will notice Steve's name mentioned countless times. In actuality, the routes listed in this book are only part of his legacy. Between Steve moving to Anchorage in 1980, and his untimely death in 1999, he changed the face of Alaska rock and ice climbing forever.

If you were fortunate enough to be one of Steve's many partners, you never forgot the experience. His raw athletic talent and bold personality combined to produce near flawless climbing. His movements were secure, deliberate and purposeful, almost as if every move had been choreographed and rehearsed a hundred times; poor protection, thin, runout, desperate…he never wavered.

Steve moved to Alaska from Massachusetts in 1977 to attend UAF. After college he moved to Anchorage and began working for North Slope Telecom doing tower work. His schedule provided him the opportunity to climb full tilt during his time off. It wasn't long before he was tearing up the local scene with first ascents on both rock and ice. His passion and appetite for climbing was voracious, as was his need for available partners.

I was new to Alaska in 1988 and had the opportunity to be schooled by him. The first thing I noticed was his no-nonsense demeanor. He was the leader, and you "best not forget it." His direct nature commanded immediate respect. While climbing with Steve, there were unspoken expectations such as…have your act together, be on time, and no sniveling. If I wanted to take my lead climbing baby steps, I was to do it on my own time with my own newbie partners. He was straight forward and to the point about everything, including his opinions about life, and his animated attention to climbing details.

Roger Pollard, another one of Steve's partners, wrote a humorous article recalling a Garvey tongue-lashing during a climb when he failed to properly manage the 300' rappel ropes. Steve chortled, "If I wanted to be a Brownie mother, then I would have been a Brownie mother!" He could be a tyrant, but for good reason. The climbing with Steve was always a serious endeavor, and a lack of focus could have ended in disaster. Looking back on it now, I deeply appreciate how tough he was with me.

In addition to being an iconic climber Steve was a devoted family man. His wife, Lynne Garvey writes: *I met Steve on the shores of Lake Winnipesaukee, New Hampshire while he was home healing from a climbing injury. His exuberance for life set him apart. He took my breath away and there it began, my life with Steve. I later relocated to Alaska and began ten years of adventure. He woke every day with a love of life. I married him and followed the road less traveled, learning not only to climb, but to live every moment in the present. Our life was filled with three children, climbing, camping, skiing and traveling together. We made first ascents of Family Matters with son Kyle and Marital Bliss - aptly named for how he intertwined our lives. Climbing was in his blood, the fire in his soul. It was his lifeline and later that passion would sadly end his life. I thank the stars above for the time I had with him. He was a gift to us all!*

Thanks to Steve, Alaska crags and canyons are studded with visionary routes on which we can challenge ourselves for years to come. For those of us who's lives he touched, we are all the better for it.
- Jay and Kathy Rowe, Jan. 2020

BPR Wall PM 70min

Approach:

The BPR Wall includes a classic Hatcher Pass approach at over an hour. Although you can see the wall from the parking lot, it is also easy to see the hills and rocks which are necessary to bypass. Start by parking after the American Alpine Club's (AAC) outhouse and walk a bit up the road, looking for a trail leading off to the left toward the Fairangel Lakes. There are many trails in this area so try and find a well-used one and not create any more. Follow trails toward Fairangel Valley, going through the large boulder field in the pass; stay to the right of the lakes. Once above the boulder field, head direct right toward the BPR Wall, which will be located about halfway up the mountain. There is not much of a developed trail toward the rock currently; however, if one starts to be created, please follow this trail and not blast your own way, killing the tundra.

Area:

The BPR Wall is named after Brian Paul Reagan who was killed while riding in a small plane in 2000. He was on his way to be a volunteer park ranger in Denali National Park when the crash occurred. This section of rock was dedicated to him by his friends who developed the wall. The area is not that large but includes some stellar crack climbing in a beautiful arena. BPR Wall is characterized by great cracks and a beautiful setting. I recommend using tape on *The Pipeline*, as the two finger jam that you use to pull over the roof likes to take skin. The height of the rock above the valley also gives a slight sense of exposure. Generally great rock with cracks of different sizes and difficulty will give all a healthy sense of accomplishment once the day is done. The anchoring situation could use some cleanup, a few more bolts would help, right now it is a concoction of ropes and slings around boulders.

1 Genep de Alaska 5.9r
Trad rack, Pitons, Sling anchor
Around and left of the main wall, a thin seam follows to a fixed piton 5 meters up. Hook right onto the face and then continue back left of the wall. There are a few pitons on this route to help with runouts.
FA: Chris Bouch, Zach Schlosar

2 The Growler 5.8 ☆☆☆☆☆ 25m
Gear to 3", Sling anchor
Start in a crack under the large rectangular roof in the left most corner. A few good areas for placements down low to protect in case of an early fall. Follow the corner to an overhanging crack veering left. Once over the lip, follow the obvious crack direct. There are several different cracks which you can veer to on this route, and all go at around 5.8 or 5.9. This is beautiful crack climbing on a high face, which gives a nice sense of exposure. Bring slings to make an anchor on rocks at the top and a good selection of medium/large cams for the climb.
FA: Tom Sardy, Zach Schlosar

3 The Pipeline 5.11b/r ☆☆☆☆ 25m
1 bolt, Gear to 2", 1 bolt + Slings anchor
Start on an easy face to the overhanging rectangular roof. This route climbs the obvious crack near the center. Pull the lip with fingers into a "Thank God" hand crack, then thank the mountain gods. Climb through ledges to a face with 1 bolt at the crux. The ledge above the bolt is the last place for pro. There are rocks at the top to sling and 1 bolt for the anchor.
FA: Zach Schlosar, Andy Hoyt

4 75 Cents to Ride 5.10a ☆☆☆ 25m
1 piton, Gear to 2", Sling anchor
Begin just right of the rectangular roof on the arete. Follow a small crack right then up to a small ledge. Hook right onto the obvious hand crack. Follow into a corner past a piton and continue to a large slingable rock on the top.
FA: Zach Schlosar, Chris Bouch, 07.2000

On June 19, 2000, Brian Paul Reagan was on his way to begin mountain patrol in Denali National Park when the Cessna 185 he was riding in crashed during a storm on the west side of Yentna Glacier. He was 27 years old. The plane crash also claimed the lives of pilot Don Bowers (52), and perspective rangers Cale Shaffer (25), and Adam Kolff (27).

LOWER LANE WALLS

	CRAG	SUN & HIKE	ROUTES	RANGE	PAGE
1	The Jungle Gym	AM 20min	9	5.7-5.9+	94
2	The Monolith	15min	21	5.4-5.12a	96

While there are only two walls located in the Lower Lane Walls area, they are probably going to see plenty of traffic. The Monolith is already one of the more trafficked areas in all of Hatcher Pass and is most likely going to continue being so. Each area has its own approach, but they both start from the end of Archangel Road. Continue walking the road after the gate at the end, and you will eventually end up at the Monolith. If you are going to the Jungle Gym, you can cross the river anywhere that looks like you can hop the rocks across, then just head to the cliff as there is no good established trail yet.

The Jungle Gym AM 20min

Approach:
Park at the end of Archangel Road near the gate and continue the walk on the road past the gate. After a few hundred meters the brush will thin out on your left as you are nearly directly in line with the cliff. Walk through the brush and directly toward the cliff, staying primarily on the grass and off of the boulder field. Since this area is new there is no definitive trail yet.

Area:
This crag is a great place to go if you just want to do some easy clipping of bolts and gear placements, although the anchors and bolts may be suspect. Some of the hardware is a bit funky, as you will find quarter inch bolts and oddly placed pitons for anchors; but overall it is a good area. The sun leaves it early, however, so it's a great place to go in the morning.

1 Stairway to Heaven 5.8 ☆☆☆ 20m
Gear to 1", 1 bolt + 1 piton anchor
Start on the left face of the formation on thin cracks with stopper placements. Continue on easy ledges, higher than you would expect, to the same anchor as *Highway to Hell.*
FA: Andy Hoyt

2 Highway to Hell 5.7 ☆☆ 21m
Gear to 2", 1 bolt + 1 piton anchor
Move inside the big corner on good gear and out left of the upper roof. Watch for drag from under the roof as you follow the arete to the upper anchor.
FA: Andy Hoyt

3 Could Be Better 5.8 ☆☆☆ 20m
Gear to 3", 1 bolt + 1 piton anchor
Climbs a crack to the left of the bolted face. Could use more traffic to clean it off and will improve with time. Finish the arete to a high anchor that, for some reason, uses a piton.
FA: Andy Hoyt

4 As Good As It Gets 5.9 ☆☆☆☆ 20m
4 bolts, Gear to 1", 2 bolt anchor
A great climb with a blocky start on gear to a clean upper face. Fun sustained moves on the upper face lead you to a strangely bolted anchor.
FA: Andy Hoyt

5 Could Be Worse 5.8 ☆ 20m
Gear to 2", 2 bolt anchor
This climb needs a lot of cleaning and really would only deserve two stars if it was. It follows a crack as it goes right to a grass ledge. Follow ledges and thin gear to use the same anchor for *As Good As It Gets*.
FA: Andy Hoyt

6 New School 5.9 ☆☆☆ 20m
4 bolts, Gear to .75", 2 bolt anchor
A fun arete that starts with a tricky move on a hard to see sidepull. Gear between the first and last two bolts.
FA: Alison Ford

7 Old School 5.8 ☆☆ 18m
Gear to 2", 2 bolt anchor
The original climb on the cliff. A blocky corner leads to a fist crack with possible offwidth moves. Bring several #3's. Ends at the same anchor as *New School*.

8 The RP Boys 5.9+ ☆☆☆ 25m
Gear to 2", 2 bolt anchor
Climb to a hand crack that splits the first roof and then great finger locks up the face to finish on the left edge of the upper roof on small gear. Bring stoppers.
FA: Andy Hoyt

9 Randy's Roof 5.9 ☆☆☆☆ 25m
6 bolts, 2 bolt anchor
A great face to a juggy roof. Split the roof on big holds with fun airy moves. Finish high on the cliff.
FA: Andy Hoyt, Josh Varney

The Monolith 15min

Approach:
Park at the end of Archangel Road near the gate and continue the walk on the road as it turns into a trail near the mine. This is a short walk and as long as you stay direct toward the Monolith you will run right into it.

Area:
The Monolith has a storied past since it is one of the most obvious walls in the valley, a large block of granite poking out in the middle of the valley with a mining road leading right up to it. There used to be a cabin that was burned down, and some fingers were pointed at climbers. Some routes in the area probably go back to the 1960's or 70's. Most others were put up in the 80's and early 90's. Either way, climbing has been happening on this rock for at least 30 years. This wall has the largest concentration of routes within Hatcher Pass, and there are difficulties at all levels. It is a great place to spend a day of cragging, although there is little development left on the cliff.

Private Property: Do not damage, burn, or otherwise destroy anything you find in this area. Hopefully, we can continue to climb on this land without having to fight with land owners. This has been a problem in the past so let's not make things worse. The Monolith is an excellent example of private property issues that have occurred in Hatcher Pass. Currently it is probably the most climbed area in Hatcher, yet it sits on private property. The route *A Bullet From Fritz* was named after the miner (Fritz), who used to own the property, sent a few shots from his shotgun as a warning to the climbers who had just finished the route. Every few years someone seems to come out and claim ownership of the land and ask that all the climbers leave. Remember, respect their wishes if someone asks you to leave; they may just own the place.

1 Chickenhead 5.4 ☆☆ 23m

Gear to 1", 2 bolt rap anchor

This is the access route for *A Bullet From Fritz.* There is an anchor here where the route used to continue to the top right anchors. It is an easy grass ledge so there is not much reason for the continuation, especially since the upper anchors require a 2 rope rappel.

Crackhead Var. 5.7: Climb above *Chickenhead* then move left to meet with the crack system of *A Bullet From Fritz.* (38m)

2 A Bullet From Fritz 5.11a ☆☆☆ 30m

6 bolts, Gear to 2", 2 bolt anchor

Start on the left side of the *Chickenhead* slab using gear for protection. Climb to the base of a grass ledge which climbs up right. From the base of the grass ledge climb along the slab with bolts to a good crack system with decent protection. Climb the cracks to a 2 bolt anchor. Walkoff or double rope rappel.

Note: This route was practiced on toprope and about to be led when the landowner came and shot off his gun in the direction of the climbers.

FA: David Whitelaw, Amy Johnson 06.25.1988

3 Local Motion 5.7 ☆☆☆ 45m

6 bolts, Gear to .5", 2 bolt rap anchor

Climb the right side of the *Chickenhead* slab on the left portion of the wall. Very runout slab that has lots of ground fall potential were something to go wrong. Climb past an anchor on the left and continue up to a higher anchor. Parts of this climb can feel harder than 5.7 especially when wet. Often done only on bolts. Walkoff or a mandatory double rope rappel. It is very common to hear of close calls on this route. Don't mess around, just tie a knot in the end of your rope.

FA: David Whitelaw, Amy Johnson 6.25.1988

4 Left Troll 5.7 ☆☆☆ 40m

Gear to 3", 1 bolt + Gear anchor

Climb to the right of the grass ramp into the corner below the roof. There are several cracks on the right. Climb up the cracks to a great flake and out the right of the roof. Bring a larger 5" or 6" cam if you wish to protect the final moves. Belay from the top of the large block and marvel at its ability to stay put. Continue on a crack above to meet with the anchors for *Local Motion* or rappel from the single bolt (30m not recommended). Bring two ropes for the rappel.

Slab Left 5.10a ☆☆ 22m

r to 2", 3 bolt anchor

Climb left of *Zig Zag* on the slab to the first bolt. Place gear in the *Zig Zag* crack if you want to eliminate runouts. Climb up and left to the next bolt then direct to a small ledge. Meet with *The Slot* here then go up right to the anchors.

6 Zig Zag 5.9 ☆☆☆ 22m

Gear to 2", 3 bolt anchor

Start on a thin crack which zig zags its way up the slab face. Stay in the crack until it meets with *The Slot* then continue to the anchors. Placing gear can seem like an oddity at times, stoppers are helpful.

7 The Slot 5.7 ☆☆☆☆☆ 21m

Gear to 3", 3 bolt anchor

Walk to the right portion of this slab. There is a crack which quickly goes to a large seemingly detached flake. Move left along a slab ramp and then join another crack which goes up right to the anchors. This is a really good beginner lead.

8 Just One More 5.8 ☆☆

1 bolt, Gear to 3", 3 bolt anchor

4 meters right and slightly uphill of *The Slot* is this broken crack in a slab going up to a single bolt. Move left and meet with *The Slot* to use the same anchors.

Uniqueka Gilbert climbing Local Motion with Shasta Gray on belay in 2009 (Courtesy John Borland)

9 Freedom Roof 5.10a/r ☆☆☆☆ 40m

4 bolts, 2 bolt anchor

An enjoyable new route which starts on the anchors for *The Slot*. Climb left then up a slab to a bolt. There are only 2 bolts before the roof and 2 more after, but they are on relatively easy ground. It is a runout but doesn't feel much like one. Definitely a "one move wonder," only pulling the lip makes this a 5.10 climb. Rappel to *The Slot* and then to the ground.

FA: Ben Chriswell, Skine Boynton 07.04.2006

10 American Slab Dance 5.10c ☆☆☆ 27m

6 bolts, Gear to .75", 2 bolt rap anchor

You can access this pitch by first climbing *The Slot* and moving right or the first pitch of *Orangutan Overhang*. Make a gear anchor near the base of the pitch, which is just to the left of *Orangutan Overhang Pitch 2*. Follow up the slab using bolts on small nubbins. Easy crack and moderate climbing lead through the upper wall. Rappel back to the ledge and walk right for the rappel station back to the ground.

FA: Chris Williams, Eric Wickenheiser

11 Orangutan Overhang 5.9+, 5.9+ ☆☆☆☆ 60m

Pitch 1: 5.9+, Gear to 1", Gear anchor ☆☆☆☆ 29m

Climb several small roofs from a corner along a crack to a large grassy ledge. From this ledge you can set up a nice gear belay or continue on *Pitch 2* for the rest of the route. If you continue on, it will take two ropes for the rappel. If you lower off the grass ledge walk right and there is an anchor over the top of the large corner at the end of the ledge.

Pitch 2 aka Upper Zig Zag: 5.9+, Gear to 2", 2 bolt rap anchor ☆☆☆☆ 31m

Start in a relatively clean looking corner directly above *Orangutan Overhang*. Climb past the chockstone and at right of the roof. To make this more pleasant instead of going direct into the chimney, climb out right to a nice crack. Go direct from there to the anchors. Walkoff rappel to the grass ledge and walk to the rappel anchor on the right. A 70m makes it to this ledge.

12 Too Much Fun For You 5.10b ☆☆☆☆☆ 55m

15 bolts, 2 bolt rap anchor

A long route with sustained 5.10 climbing, some bolts will feel runout. Start on the slab and climb two bolts to a roof. Move out left of the roof and then move right once over the lip. Chickenhead and face climbing direct to the anchors. Some runouts could be filled with S/M cams or stoppers. The climb ends at the top of the cliff. Rappel to the anchors for *Orangutan Overhang Pitch 1* or do a double rope rappel. A walkoff is also possible.

FA: John Trautwein 1992

⑬ Shot on Sight 5.10d ☆☆ 55m

There is a 2 bolt anchor 2 meters below a better 2 bolt anchor. All climbs which go to the top and share this anchor will have these 2 bolts from the lower anchor added into the bolt count.

Var 1: 9 bolts, 3 pitons, Gear to 2", 2 bolt rap anchor
Begin with the same start as *Too Much Fun For You* and climb to the overhang. Move right along a large scary block until in the large corner that goes to the top. Follow it.

Var. 2: 7 bolts, 3 pitons, Gear to 2", 2 bolt rap anchor
Climb *Easy Rider* to a grassy ledge. There is one bolt on the face in front of this climb. Climb up the bolt and move into the corner.

The main climb has a second variation from the bolt after *Vein of Gold*. Move right across a face to a flake facing away from the climb. Move onto this flake and climb until it runs out back near the corner. Continue on the corner until the anchor. Double rope rappel or climb out and walkoff.

FA: Jay Rowe, Scott Mignery

14 Easy Rider 5.7 ☆☆

Gear to 3", No anchor

This climb ascends the far left arete of this lower portion up a wide crack. It is an easy way to access *Vein of Gold* or *Shot on Sight Var. 2*. There are no anchors, however you can go up the ramp to the right for the same anchor as *Black Wall*, otherwise it pretty much ends on a grassy ledge.

15 Vein of Gold 5.10c ☆☆☆☆☆ **55m**

4 bolts, Gear to 2", 2 bolt anchor

Climb *Checkered Dog* and walk across the grass ledge. There is a orangish color section of rock with a left leaning crack that looks very clean. That's it alright! Move left with the thin finger crack until in the corner of the large dihedral. You can also go right of the thin crack into a another great crack on the face. Continue to the same anchors as *Shot on Sight*. Mandatory TCU's in the crux.

FA: Roger Pollard, David Whitelaw 1987

16 Checkered Dog 5.9 ☆☆☆☆

Gear to 1", 2 bolt rap anchor

Start low on the slab and climb up into an enjoyable crack. Usually more dry than *Black Wall* and definitely more entertaining. Use fingers and hand jams through the well protected crux. Once on the ledge move up right for the anchors above the formation or continue on to *Vein of Gold*.

FA: David Whitelaw, Roger Pollard, Amy Johnson

17 Black Wall 5.8 ☆☆

Gear to 2", 2 bolt rap anchor

Start in a broken crack and move left. Often wet and muggy midway through the crack system. Continue up to a small roof, pull over the lip and move up right to the anchors.

FA: Steve Garvey

18 Spring Fling 5.8 ☆☆☆

1 bolt, Gear to 2", 2 bolt rap anchor

Climb up a grassy ledge to a very short corner. Move left out to a crack which angles right. Climb this enjoyable crack system to a bolt. Continue through the corner direct to the anchors.

FA: Tom Evans, Greg Bombeck, Roger Pollard

19 Unknown 5.10b / 5.12a ☆☆

3 bolts, Gear to 2", 2 bolt rap anchor

Start on the face just left of *Flakey*. Climb past two bolts to a small lip. Move left to a thin crack and climb direct to the last bolt. Meets with *Spring Fling* to follow the corner to the anchor. Climbing the bolts direct make this route about 5.12a.

FA: Paul Turecki

20 Flakey 5.9+ ☆☆☆

Gear to 2", 2 bolt rap anchor

Climb a short face to multiple flakes. Move left at the lip and continue on a crack to the anchors.

21 Inside Right 5.7 ☆☆☆

Gear to 3", 2 bolt rap anchor

Climb into a small chimney and then to a large corner. The crack here is pretty enjoyable and it is great to have a 5.7 with a roof. Move right with the crack then pull over the lip and continue the crack left to the anchors. There is a single bolt above the anchor that can be used as an exit bolt if you wish to end at the top of the cliff (5.6).

JJ Brooks on the classic line, Roger's Roof (p.107) in 1989. (Courtesy Jay Rowe)

UPPER LANE WALLS

	CRAG	SUN & HIKE	ROUTES	RANGE	PAGE
1	Lane Wall	AM 80min	3	5.6-5.8	105
2	Roger's Roof	90min	2	5.10b-5.11+	107
3	Bear's Den & Midnight Rock	AM 100min	5	5.8-5.10d	108

The Upper Lane Walls area is located further down the trail past the Monolith and is a beautiful hike in its own. This area used to be a great place to spend a few nights, as there was a decent hut at the back of the valley. That was changed in the last few years when it was burned down. It seems to be the fate of all the Hatcher Pass huts, as they've slowly been disappearing over the last decade. There are only a few areas in this book, but this valley may have the best concentration of single pitch cracks as anywhere in Hatcher Pass. It's a big trip out but worth it for those willing to explore.

Jay Rowe

Jay Rowe has been an active Alaska climber since moving here in 1988 when he and his wife Kathy were married. He learned how to rock climb during his college years in Washington State and has made first ascent contributions both locally and in the Alaska Range.

During the early 90s, Jay, along with a host of others, made a number of first ascents on the Seward Highway, Hatcher Pass, and The Wedge. These experiences fueled his desire to establish longer first ascent routes in the Alaska Range. His early first ascents include a pair of grade 5 rock climbs on the East Face of Peak 3596 in the Deep Water Bay area of Prince William Sound. After this, he turned his attention to the Alaska Range where he has been active since his first trip in 1993. A list of his first ascent routes include the East Face of the Tusk, the South Buttress of Sugar Tooth, and first ascent of both Coffee and Mocha spires. In 2013, after several attempts spread out over a 20 year period, Jay finally reached the summit of Broken Tooth via a major variation to the West Ridge Route. This climb also completed his quest to climb routes on all five of the formations of the Moose's Tooth massif. He returned to the Coffee Glacier in 2020 and added a pair of new routes on Coffee and Mocha Spires. He writes, "For me, alpine climbing represents an unmatched level of challenge, uncertainty, and thrill. I consider it a privilege to have been able to visit many magnificent untouched places in Alaska."

Jay lives in Anchorage with his wife Kathy. They are both retired educators and are busy enjoying all the wonders Alaska has to offer.

Top Right: Jay on the West Ridge variation of Broken Tooth 2013. (Courtesy Peter Haeussler)
Bottom Right: Jay on East Ridge Broken Tooth attempt 2011. (Courtesy Micha Miller)
Bottom: Jay in his element in the Alaska Range. (Courtesy Daniel Barton)

Lane Wall AM 80min

Approach:
Located directly above the old Lane Hut site, this wall is easy to access. Hike toward the Monolith and take a well-worn right off-shoot after a few minutes. This takes you higher up the mountain before hooking left and heading toward the pass. Follow through the pass and continue in the valley until it hooks right toward the Lane Glacier. There used to be a hut located next to some very large enticing boulders, but it was burned down within the last few years. The older photo below shows a small portion of the old hut. This wall is located in a jumble of cliffs at the end of the valley.

Area:
The Lane Hut used to be a decent place to wait for the rain to die down, while running outside to get a few laps in. However, the Lane Hut has since burned down, so there is no longer the opportunity. It was burned down by the park service as they deemed it a safety hazard. There are not many huts left around for your casual user as most have now burned. It's an unfortunate loss of resource and history due to lack of care. If you visit any of the remaining structures, please spend some time improving it before you leave. Maybe we can keep them a bit longer. I would not make the effort simply for this area unless you are going to do more than I have listed here. The climbs don't see much traffic so they are normally mossy areas with a splattering of lichen. More traffic could improve them but it would take quite a bit. As an added bonus, there is a very large boulder just next to the old Lane Hut site that has a few problems on it. It has a single bolt on the top and the easy and obvious route is about 5.6. It was put up by Dave Staeheli and friends; they called it *Thunder Road*.

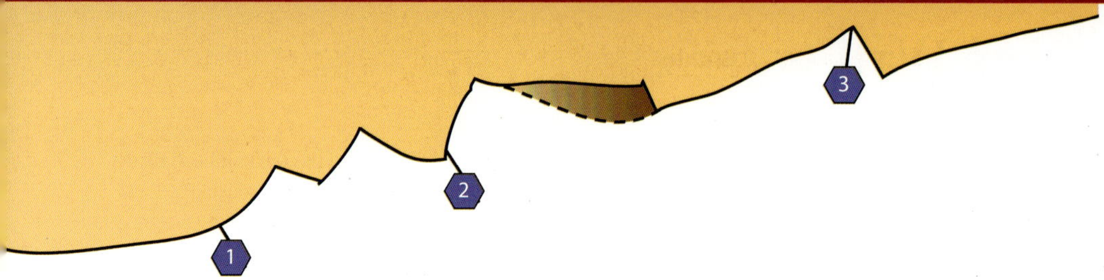

1 A Lady Named Lew 5.6 ☆☆ **32m**

Gear to 3", 2 bolt anchor

Starts on a nice flat grass ledge with a small clean face. Climb easy unprotected moves over the face or move right over the top of the face and climb meandering cracks interspersed with grass ledges. Continue going up and along loose blocks to a large grass ledge. There is a semi-blank face on the right. Move around left of the face and walk over the top of it to the anchors for *Lane Game*. Best to belay from here and walk right off the route or rappel.

FA: Jay Rowe, Kathy Rowe, Erik Skye, Tom Elton

The Lane Wall is more of a distraction than a worthy climbing area. If you have the time, head further up the valley where better climbing awaits.

2 Lane Game 5.8 ☆

Gear to 3", 2 bolt anchor

Follow up a section of mossy cracks and loose blocks until a small overhang. Move right along the overhang to a crack which goes direct. Moss and loose rock abound until the anchor. Could use lots of cleaning. Crawl up and left at the top for the anchor.

3 Fresh Fish 5.7

Gear to 2", No anchor

Gets little traffic and has no anchors. Climb up a short crack to a large ledge and move left into moss city. Move up along this crack to multiple ledges. Walkoff the route right.

Roger's Roof 90min

Approach:
Hike toward the Monolith and take a well-worn right off-shoot after a few minutes. This takes you higher up the mountain before hooking left and heading toward the pass. Follow through the pass and continue in the valley until it hooks right toward the Lane Glacier. Continue following the valley as it curves to the right, but stay on the left side and begin ascending toward the pass. This wall is about 10 minutes from the Lane Wall on the left side. Cross the boulders to the wall.

Area:
Cracks are abundant in this area and *Roger's Roof (5.11+)* is one of the most obvious. *Roger's Roof* was first discovered as a climbing route by Roger Pollard. Although he never ascended the crux, he did get really close and came out with some good recommendations for those who would follow him. The first redpoint of *Roger's Roof* came from J.J. Brooks in 1991. *Roger's Roof* is also known as *The Jolt Roof.*

As with other crags in this area, there are routes nearby that are not listed in this guidebook. The area requires a sense of exploration as well as solid trad leading skills, as you won't find many bolts in this valley, and the ones that do exist may be older and in need of replacement.

1 Lost in the Bush 5.10b ☆☆☆☆
Gear to 4", Gear anchor
Walk/Scramble the grass left of *Roger's Roof* until a right angling crack. Move along this until there is a solid obvious fist crack going direct up the wall. Walkoff the route.
FA: Paul Turecki, J.J. Brooks 06.1988

2 Roger's Roof 5.11+ ☆☆☆☆ 35m
Gear to 4", Sling anchor
This is the obvious crack which splits the face. Here is Rogers advice for this climb: "rack the left side." Bring some TCU's for after the roof and a nut tool to clean the upper crack.
FA: J.J. Brooks, Paul Turecki, Jay Rowe

The Bear's Den & Midnight Rock AM 100min

Approach:
One of the longest approaches in this book. Begin at the end of Archangel Road and hike toward the Monolith. After about 5-10 minutes a trail will hook right and make a long left arch along the mountain to the pass. This is an easier trail to take, but you can also access the pass by going along the side of the Monolith. Continue the well-worn trails following the valley floor as it hooks right toward the Lane Wall. Follow along the trail for the Bomber Traverse heading toward the next pass. The rocks are not yet visible. You will pass Lane Wall and Roger's Roof on the left. Continue along the trail until you are almost at the pass. The Bear's Den is about halfway up the mountain on the left and looks like a square leaning left. Midnight Rock faces the Bear's Den area and is located just left across a small rock gully.

Area:
Those who have visited the Lane Hut may have found the hand written sheets of paper that tell about the Bear's Den and several other areas around the Lane Hut. Those sheets were written by Jay Rowe in 1992 and remained in the hut until it burned down. All the routes located here were put up within a year of each other.
Although the approach is long, it is always worth a trip into the area. This valley has the most cracks I have seen in one area in Hatcher Pass. Many have been done, although there is little information about them but there are still a great amount of possibilities for first ascents. There are new anchors on top of each climb making it a lot easier to safely belay and lower.

The Bear's Den

There are a great deal of cracks to the right of this area, which would be much harder climbs, but look like fun for anyone wanting to give it a try. The rock is generally solid and all the climbs can be done without rappelling as there is a very easy walkoff down the back side.

1 Turecki's Ten 5.9 ☆☆☆☆ **16m**

Gear to 3", 2 bolt rap anchor

The second crack left of the large corner, climb to a few small roofs and moves onto a small ledge. The route moves right into the side pull crack with chickenheads thrown throughout the route for extra enjoyment. Instead of going through the large roof crack, move left along the chickenheads and meet back with the crack once on the ledge; this could make it harder. There is a new anchor on top of the route to use.

FA: Paul Turecki, Jay Rowe 07.1989

2 Straight Eight 5.9+ ☆☆☆☆ **15m**

Gear to 4", 2 bolt rap anchor

Begin in the first crack left of the corner and climb direct to the top. A great clean fist and hand crack. This route now has its own anchor.

FA: Jay Rowe, Paul Turecki 07.1989

Tara Storter on Fine Nine (Courtesy Todd Fisher)

3 Fine Nine 5.9+ ☆☆☆☆

Gear to 2", 2 bolt rap anchor

Start in the obvious corner crack which would initially appear to have blank feet. Climb the cracks that meander along in the corner.

FA: Jay Rowe, J.J. Brooks, Doug White 06.1990

Midnight Rock

Enjoyable area with a finger crack to a roof and the only bolts you'll find on a climb in this area. There are second pitch possibilities and some webbing strewn throughout the area but I was not able to find any information on them.

4 Midnight Madness 5.10d
3 bolts, Gear to 2", 2 bolt anchor
Climb up shattered cracks to a grass ledge. Climb in the corner on a finger crack to the roof. Traverse right out of the roof onto a bolted face. Climb direct to the anchor.
FA: Jay Rowe, Scott Mignery 06.1990

5 Midnight Rider 5.8
Gear to 3", 2 bolt anchor
Just right of the corner system around on the face is a crack system that goes near direct to the top. Climb that crack intermixed with flakes to the anchor the same as *Midnight Madness*.
FA: Scott Mignery, Jay Rowe

Ballad of a Dead Pinto - AKA Dasher by Dave Nyman
Well I saddled me up a little yeller pinto, she was a purty little gal (yeah she was).
Now I took that little yeller pinto up to Hatcher Pass, that Hatcher Pass
Gitty up little pinto, Gitty up horya
Well I rolled me a big stogy, She were a big one at that
Well I left it on her seat
That poor little pinto, she fried in the heat, she died at my feet.
Now she lies dead – in front of that good ol' cabin off the street
Now Tim said I aint ever be sadder in grief.
I've left that Hatcher Pass and bought me a Cadillac Deville.
Now its twenty year later and I got me a gal. Her name is Pintella
When I say her name I call her "Little Pinto".
Now there's some snivelin' boy his name is Sweeney.
Ya he's a dog so I've heard.
Now I hear he's a thinkin' of robbin' the grave.
Gonna take that little pinto and drag her away and drag her away.
Now I be takin' that Deville down to the Hatcher Hill
I be lookin' for Sweeney
I be lookin' for a tight rope.

Melissa Kochanowsky climbing Titanic (5.6) on the Nugget Boulder (p.121) with El Potrero Chico, Mexico guidebook author Frank Madden, on belay.

LOWER REED VALLEY

	CRAG	SUN & HIKE	ROUTES	RANGE	PAGE
1	The Crack Garden	60min	20	5.5-5.10c	114
2	Nugget Boulder	50min	5	5.6-5.11c	120
3	Snowbird Slab	50min	16	5.6-5.10d	122
4	The Broken Ones	AM 65min	1	5.12a	128
5	Devil's Gully	70min	5	5.8-5.10a	130
6	Inferno Wall	75min	9	5.8-5.11c	132

Reed Valley is also located down Archangel Road. It is not at the end of the road, however, and has its own little parking lot that is often beyond crowded. Drive down Archangel Road 2.2 miles from the turn off of the main road. Once you have crossed the main bridge at about 2 miles, the parking lot will be soon after on the right. There is room here for at least 15 cars if everyone is parking thoughtfully, although it's easy to park on top of a large rock. Parking is no longer free so bring $5 for a pass or continue further down the road and park. This is also the best access for the Snowbird Glacier.

LOWER REED VALLEY CONT...

	CRAG	SUN & HIKE	ROUTES	RANGE	PAGE
7	Pulp Culture Wall	80min	6	5.7-5.10a	135
8	Fatal Attraction Wall	90min	3	5.10b-5.11a	138
9	Dermatologist Dream	AM 70min	9	5.7r-5.12a	142
10	Birds of Prey	AM 75min	7	5.8-5.11a	146
11	Reed Creek Wall	AM 65min	9	5.7-5.11b	148
12	Zydeco Wall	PM 65min	4	5.8-5.10a	151
13	The Barnyard	AM 75min	6	5.8-5.10a	153

The Crack Garden 60min

Approach:
Park at the Reed Lakes parking lot and begin the hike along the main trail, keeping an eye on the cliff at your left. You'll end up going past the cliff after nearly a mile and head left through some brush into a clearing. From here it helps to go toward the river bed due to the height of the brush and greenery. It is easier to walk up the river bed when it is dry and then hook left when you are level with the cliff. This is a long uphill hike that will take its own bit of energy before getting to some great climbing.

Area:
We'd all looked at this area but it always seemed like more of a trek to get to than Snowbird Slab and the other areas near the gap, so we saved it for another day. It looks like it would have been worth it, however, as Galen and crew found some excellent crack climbs with some unusual consistency for Hatcher. There are some great cracks in this area with some excellent moderates such as *The Apology Foot Rub (5.8)* and the inventively named *Tritonian Yeti Physics (5.8)*. The crux of the crag is getting there.

A single 70m rope should work for most of the crag; 60m ropes are not ideal here. There are also multiple toprope anchors on top of the Crack Garden area that help to reduce any long rappels. The routes can be long rope stretchers so always tie knots in the end when rappelling or lowering climbers.

Noah Samuelson on The Apology Foot Rub during an early ascent. (Courtesy Galen Vansant)

Crack Garden

The Crack Garden is the center of the cliff and the main area of concentration of climbs. When arriving at the cliff from the main trail, follow the trail along the base passing Garden Party Buttress and the Hanging Garden.

1 Chickenheads on a Chopping Board 5.5 ☆☆ **38m**

Gear to 3", Gear anchor

From Crack Garden this route ascends a slab high and left of the formation. Scramble grass that is steep enough in its own right to be a pitch and head to the base of a slab with a big crack in it. Follow cracks with good chickenheads and sometimes mediocre gear. After topping out walk the grass direct to another small rock face with a little roof. Under the roof there is a crack for an anchor. Walkoff the route to the right of the formation coming back around *Garden Party*. A good beginner lead for the Hatcher experience as it includes gear anchors, steep scrambles, and walkoffs.

FA: Ryan Sims, Galen Vansant

2 Gateway Crack 5.7 ☆☆ **31m**

Gear to 2:", 2 bolt rap anchor

A variation to *Tritonian Yeti Physics*. From the first ledge halfway up the route, move left passing the trident crack and climb the leftmost crack on the face. End at the same anchor.

FA: Galen Vansant, Isaac Davis

3 Tritonian Yeti Physics 5.8 ☆☆☆

Gear to 2", 2 bolt rap anchor

Climb the left most crack on the lower fa left on the first large ledge to a crack shaped like an upside down trident. Climb the flaring fun with enjoyable chickenheads thrown in.

FA: Galen Vansant, Rick Roth, Kiersten Johnson

4 Turf War 5.9 ☆☆☆☆ **35m**

1 bolt, Gear to 3", 2 bolt rap anchor

This admittedly contrived line is actually pretty enjoyable. Start between *Apology Foot Rub* and *Vertical Gardener* on criss crossing cracks. *Turf War* tries to avoid using as much of any other line as possible. Climb to the right side of the flake above and then traverse left climbing *Apology Foot Rub* for just a few feet before heading left on slabby feet around the corner. Follow the left angling thin crack and pull a slab move after the top to the traverse crack of *Caustic Community Crack*. Then clip the bolt and head right to an anchor that is not the one right in front of you near the bolt. Bring slings to keep the drag down.

FA: Galen Vansant, Ryan Sims

5 Caustic Community Crack 5.7 ☆☆☆☆ **31m**

1 bolt, Gear to 2", 2 bolt rap anchor

Climb the crack that leads to the left leaning flake and right below the left leaning crack you'll see a nice hand crack on your right. Climb the hand crack and traverse left on a ledge toward the anchor. The bolt is for *Turf War* but you'll probably use it.

FA: Galen Vansant, Ezra Samulseon, Noah Samuleson

6 The Apology Foot Rub 5.8 ☆☆☆☆☆ **35m**

Gear to 3", 2 bolt rap anchor

Start on an inset corner and follow to the flakes above. From the flake move right to the obvious splitter. One of the most consistent cracks around. From the top move right into the dihedral to an on top of the dihedral. The previous anchor was over the grass but the new anchors make it toprope-able with a 70m. Tie knots in the end of your rope when rappeling or lowering a climber.

FA: Galen Vansant, Kiersten Johnson

7 The Vertical Gardener 5.8 ☆☆☆☆ **35m**

Gear to 3", 2 bolt rap anchor

Start in a small roof corner and follow thin cracks to a triangular roof. Follow the crack system to the top of the dihedral. Shares the anchor with *The Apology Foot Rub*.

FA: Rick Roth, Galen Vansant, Kiersten Johnson

Unnamed 5.10b ☆☆☆ **33m**

2 bolts, Gear to 3", 2 bolt rap anchor

Climb a thin seam right of *Vertical Gardener* and then into an opposite facing corner. Climb the dike on the slab and then back into the crack. Uses the *Vertical Gardner* anchor and is currently best as a toprope. The lead bolt for *Accidental Corking* works as a directional for the TR.

9 Accidental Corking 5.9 ☆☆☆ **33m**

2 bolts, Gear to 3", 2 bolt rap anchor

Just left of *Smoked Bluffs*, follow a series of cracks to the moss ledge. Climb the small right facing corner to a finger crack and then a bolt. Continue to a small gear placement (yellow Alien/Metolius), ignore the couple bolts up the corner and move left out onto the slab to a bolt and then the anchor.

FA: Lang Van Dommelen, Julie Costa 2017

10 Smoked Bluffs 5.8 ☆☆☆ **35m**

3 bolts, Gear to 3", 2 bolt rap anchor

Follow the furthest right crack system on the face to a ledge. Climb the short/steep crack to another small ledge. Continue up the right margin of the formation through a couple slabby corners with 3 bolts. Exit the corner and move left to the anchor. Knot your ends if lowering the leader!

FA: Jalen Cox, Cory Barber 2017

(Courtesy Galen Vansant)

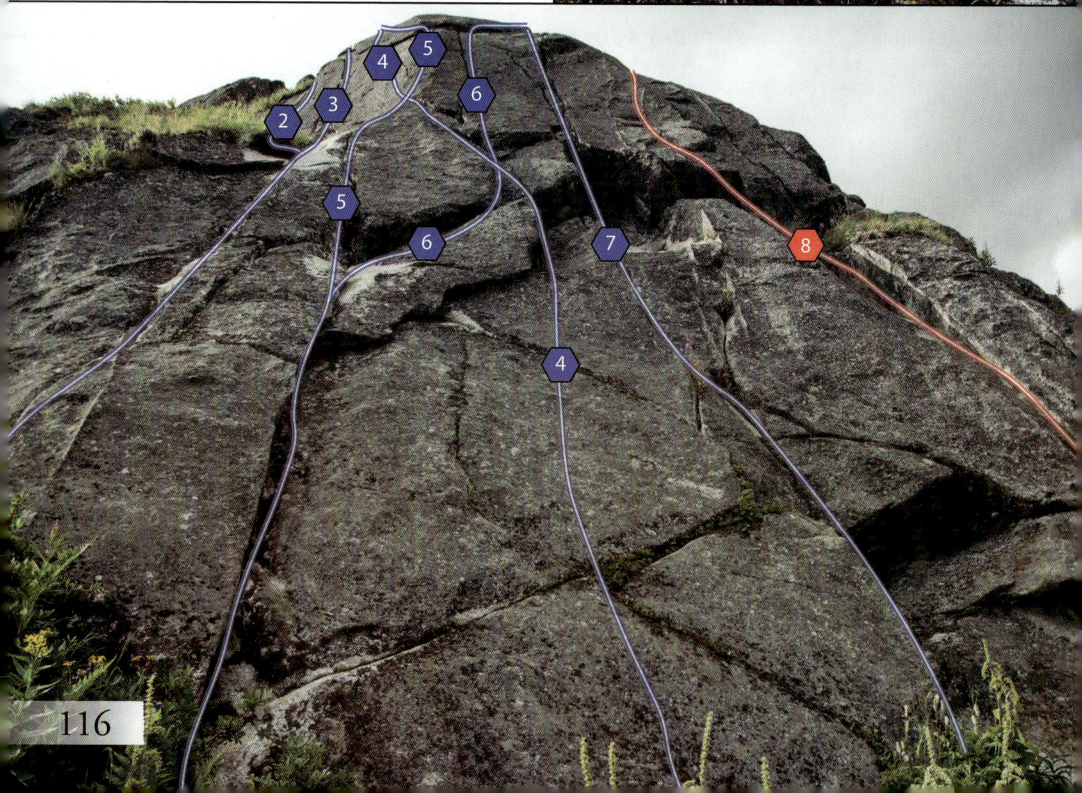

Hanging Garden

The Hanging Garden is an area just left of Garden Party Buttress and includes some excellent climbing. The best way to access these climbs is to scramble the grass just left of Garden Party Buttress and onto a grass ledge below the dihedral.

11 Adequate Fun For You 5.7 ☆☆☆ 45m

3 bolt, Gear to 3", 2 bolt anchor

One of the longest routes at the crag, located on a ledge up and left from *Prettier After Last Call.* Start up and right of the toe of the buttress. You can use a #3 camalot low to protect your belayer. Follow the fist crack with plenty of face features to a small ledge. Step left out onto the slab to a bolt. Continue past some small gear and another bolt to some broken mossy terrain at the base of the next buttress. Climb the right side to a bolt protecting the steep and reachy crux. After pulling the lip, finish up the featured slab and arete to the anchor. To walk off, from the top of the crag go down and right toward the approach gully. You don't have to go into the gully to get back to the base of the crag.

FA: Galen Vansant, Cody Boring 2018

Kelsey Gray lowering from Dick Swagger Dihedral, which starts from the same ledge as these climbs.

12 Prettier After Last Call 5.7 ☆☆ 34m

Gear to 4", 2 bolt rap anchor

Left most climb on this face. From the grass ramp climb the gardened cracks just left of *Flaked Out.* Do a couple grungy moves to a good BD #3 or #4 placement. From there head out right following a thin crack with good hand holds and slabby feet. Scramble up to the anchor.

FA: Kiersten Johnson, Drew Lindow 2018

13 Flaked Out 5.8 ☆☆☆ 33m

1 bolt, Gear to 3", 2 bolt rap anchor

From the same ledge as *Dick Swagger Dihedral* move on a short crack left up to a ledge. You can also scramble the grass left to a short corner with some gear to start the route but with bad rope drag. From the grass ledge head into cracks and follow them to a high bolt before the anchor. Thin gear. It is possible to do an exposed scramble walkoff to the right of the anchor.

14 Broad Street Bully 5.8 ☆☆☆☆ 33m

3 bolts, Gear to 3", 2 bolt rap anchor

Same start as for *Flaked Out.* From the sloping grass ramp follow intermittent cracks just right of the white patch of rock and left of the right angling hand crack of *Dick Swagger Dihedral.* Once past the overlap head for the arete. Follow the arete for a couple bolts to a horizontal crack. At the bulge move right and up to the shared bolt. Finish as for *Flaked Out.* Bring thin gear.

FA: Cory Barber, Tom Kempinski 2017

15 Dick Swagger Dihedral 5.10c ☆☆☆☆ 32m
Gear to 3", 2 bolt rap anchor
Scramble up the grass ramp on the left side of Garden Party Buttress to reach the Hanging Garden. Follow the crack up the steep dihedral directly ahead for the crux. Follow a fist crack up to another steep crux with tricky feet. There is an anchor over the ledge above. A BD#4 may be useful for the wide crack but can be bypassed.
FA: Galen Vansant, Kiersten Johnson 2016

16 Down and Dirty Dihedral 5.8 ☆☆☆☆ 25m
Gear to 3", 2 bolt rap anchor
From Hanging Garden ledge go right into the big dihedral with a right angling crack. An excellent climb. Follow as it goes up and right to the anchor of *Garden Party*.
FA: Kiersten Johnson, Galen Vansant

Garden Party Buttress

This is the first area that you will come to when approaching the wall; it is also the farthest right area at the crag. The climbs are generally mellow with long angle climbing and good stances for gear. Bring a 70m rope as a 60m will be cutting it close and may not work for all routes depending on placements.

17 Never Let You Go 5.7 ☆☆ 32m
Gear to 3", 2 bolt rap anchor
Start at the toe of the buttress and pick your way through cracks and features. There are many options for starting and climbing this route but all stay on the face and go to the high anchor.
FA: Cory Barber, Cody Boring, Galen Vansant

18 Picks and Hoes 5.8 ☆☆ 31m
Toprope, 2 bolt rap anchor
Like the next route, this one starts in a corner with a short roof, but instead of going into clean holds you move directly into a corner with moss on top. Continue along on thin climbing that could take gear when cleaned out and follow direct to the anchor staying left of *Garden Party*.

19 Garden Party 5.8 ☆☆ 31m
Gear to 3", 2 bolt rap anchor
Start in a small corner with a pointy roof. This route would be excellent if it ended halfway. From a grass ledge halfway up pull a steep move out of the small roof and finish on a high anchor. Continue following grassy ledges and corners toward the anchor.
FA: Kiersten Johnson, Galen Vansant

20 Dirty D 5.8 ☆☆☆ 31m
Gear to 3", 2 bolt rap anchor
Climb the crack system on the right edge of the buttress. Stay on the right side cracks until up high and then climb left to the anchor.
FA: Galen Vansant, Ryan Sims

Jalen Cox on the first ascent of Smoked Bluffs (p.116) at The Crack Garden. (Courtesy Galen Vansant)

Nugget Boulder 50min

Approach:
Park at the trailhead for Reed Lakes and hike the main trail to the two river bridge crossings at 1.5 miles in. Cross the bridges over the creek, and shortly after starting uphill, move right toward the small lakes. There are often signs at the intersections just after the bridges. Follow the sign that points toward the right, to the Beaver Dams. The large boulder plopped down in the tundra is Nugget Boulder.

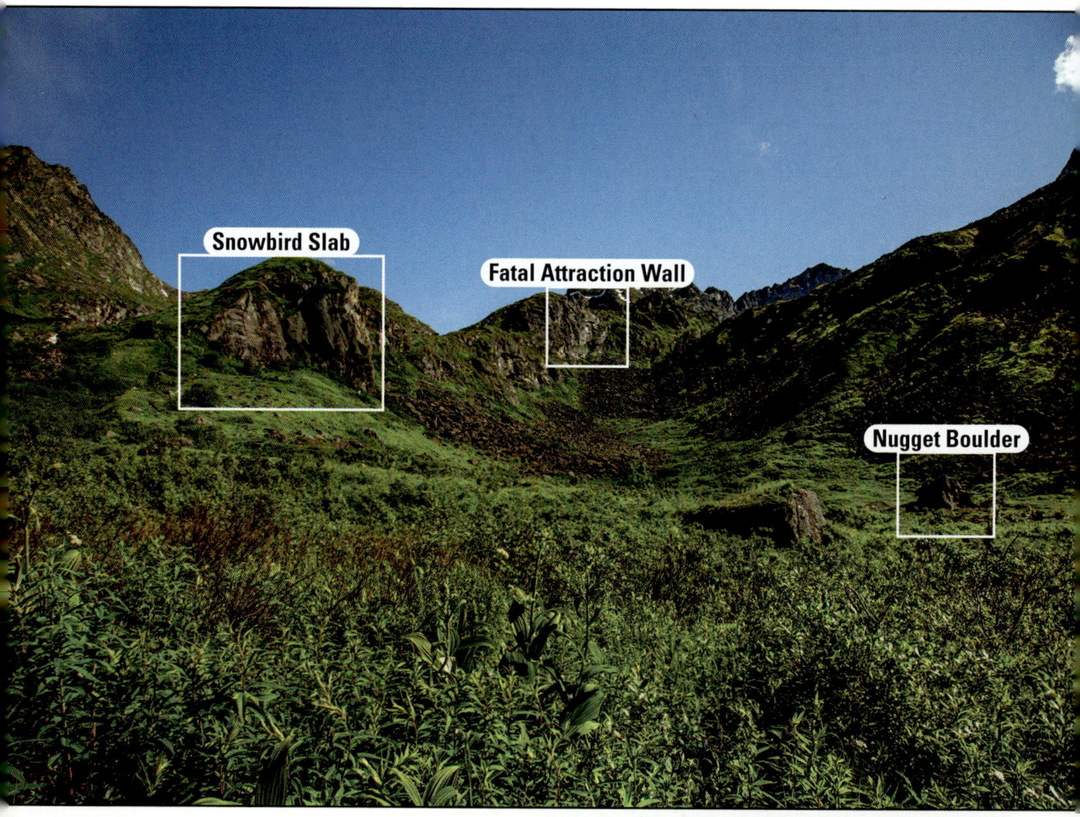

Area:
This is a great area to spend a few hours if you are short on time, although if you feel comfortable at moderate difficulties you may find this a fun highball boulder. Also a good place to end the day with some easy climbs, which is likely why it sees a surprising amount of traffic. The short but enjoyable route *Titanic (5.6)* is a great beginner lead. You can walk off any of the climbs by going to the back of the boulder and jumping to another block that split from the original. This jump gets a little more scary each year as the moss landing erodes making the angle steeper.

Frank Madden climbing Banana Show with Melissa Kochanowsky belaying on a beautiful sunny afternoon.

1 Mary Poppins 5.7 ☆☆ **9m**

3 bolts, 2 bolt rap anchor

Yeah, it's a runout, but it's a chimney. Start in the chimney and climb out right after the second bolt. Anchors for *Titanic* are the best to use. Bring 22" inch gear if you are worried about protection.

2 Unknown 5.6r ☆☆ **9m**

2 bolts, 2 bolt rap anchor

Start just left of *Titanic* following the quartz ledges which slope left until the top. There is one odd beaten and very untrustworthy bolt near the bottom. Walk right to the anchor for *Titanic* to lower.

3 Titanic 5.6 ☆☆☆☆ **10m**

Gear to 2", 2 bolt rap anchor

Up the center of the low angle slab is this fun and pro munching finger crack. Stoppers and medium cams work great here. Excellent first trad lead. Could be done entirely on stoppers without much issue.

4 Almost Argyle 5.9 ☆☆ **11m**

Gear to 2", 2 bolt rap anchor

A variation to *Titanic*, start between a boulder and the wall around the corner from the original start. Climb up and slightly left to the large crack then follow until it meets with *Titanic*. Bring a spotter.

5 Banana Show 5.11c ☆☆☆ **11m**

Toprope, 2 bolt anchor

Climb the thin corner to an orange face. This route is a difficult climb that tests your crimper strength. Moving left toward the arete makes this about 5.11c. Moving right makes it something much harder. There is a 2 bolt anchor at the top. Toprope only for this climb.

FA: J.J. Brooks

The author setting up at the anchor for Banana Show, a short climb with a hard finish.
(Courtesy John Borland / www.morffed.com)

Snowbird Slab 50min

Approach:

Park at the Reed Lakes parking lot and hike 1.5 miles down Reed Lakes Trail. This is also the split for Snowbird Mine. Follow the trail toward Reed Lakes which goes along several small bridges and begins its hike uphill toward a seemingly low angle slab. The main trail to Reed Lakes goes directly below Snowbird Slab. If you stay on the trail you will come to the crag. There are plenty of offshoots that spread across the valley but it is best to stay on the main trail. Going off trail will continue to erode these paths further and create runoff problems. Follow the switchbacks on the very well built trail until below the cliff.

(Courtesy John Borland / morffed.com)

Area:

Slab climbing at its best, with routes ranging from 5.5 to 5.10d. There are plenty of different features on this wall to keep you busy all day long, ranging from slab climbing to crack climbing and finishing off with chickenheads. The rock is generally good for most of the climbs, although many of the crack climbs to the right of the slab, such as *Possum Kingdom*, have a tendency to be overgrown with vegetation. Beyond the established climbs, this cliff continues with decent looking rock and more possibilities abound.

This is often the busiest wall in the valley with several parties climbing on any given summer day. Due to its proximity of the trail, which goes directly under the cliff, there are often parties of less experienced climbers spending their day on these fine routes. New routes on this wall continue to grow its popularity and range. This helps keep the good routes cleaner and rebolting has made them feel more accessible. If you're new to climbing outside and looking for a few fun routes, and Snowbird Slab is too busy for your taste, then try Nugget Boulder, Reed Creek Wall, or Pulp Culture Wall.

This is the most popular climbing area in Reed Valley with the possible exception of Nugget Boulder. There are some excellent moderate climbs as well as testpieces such a Thin As Ice and Possom Kingdom, which will both test your abilities in their own way. The new climb, Rainbow Coalition, is also likely to see plenty of ascents as it is an easy climb up the face and a great introduction for new slab climbers.

1 Santa Cruz 5.7r ☆☆☆ 12m

3 bolts, 2 bolt rap anchor

Easy yet runout and short, an odd combination. Walk up a grassy vegetated ramp to the far left section of the slab. After climbing to the top, walk 2 meters right across the grass to the anchors.

FA: Amy Johnson, David Whitelaw 08.13.1988

2 Second Sally 5.6r ☆☆☆ 12m

2 bolts, Gear to .25", 2 bolt rap anchor

Same ledge as *Santa Cruz*. Climb the ledge right until you are under a bolt. Go direct through two bolts climbing on chickenheads to a 2 bolt anchor. If you fall before the first bolt expect a ride, but hey, it's a 5.6, right? Gear possible to help eliminate runouts.

FA: David Whitelaw, Amy Johnson 08.13.1988

3 Rainbow Coalition 5.6 ☆☆☆☆ 28m

9 bolts, One BD #.75 cam, 2 bolt rap anchor

This new climb was put up as an introduction into slab climbing. It is not runout (if you bring the one necessary cam) and has excellent holds right where you need them. Scramble up the grass toward *Second Sally* and then move left to a grass ledge. There is one bolt reachable from the ledge to use as a belay bolt. Move right under the bolts until its time to head up. Bring one BD #.75 or similar size to skip the runout.

FA: Kelsey Gray, Rachel Lowrance, Rene Welty 08.16.2020

4 Born to be Mild 5.7 ☆☆ 29m

5 bolts, 2 bolt rap anchor

Start in the corner and climb out over the lip for the first bolt. Follow over the slab and hook left around the bulge. 2 more bolts to the anchors.

FA: Roger Pollard

5 Tinsel Moose 5.7, 5.8r ☆☆☆ 55m

Pitch 1: 5.7, 2 bolts, Gear to 1", 2 bolt rap anchor 30m

Start in the corner and follow the right angling crack. Follow the crack until it nears the anchors for *Born to be Mild*. Hook left and use the 2 bolt anchor. Unfortunately this climb has become a mud pile at the base due to consistently running water through the climb.

Pitch 2: 5.8r, 1 bolt, Gear to .75", 2 bolt rap anchor ☆☆ 25m

Follow the slab and go direct for a big corner with stemming. There is little protection but some areas for gear. There is a 2 bolt rap anchor just right at the top of the corner. The second pitch is generally unpleasant. Double rope rappel or walkoff.

6 Thin As Ice 5.10a, 5.10a ☆☆☆☆☆ 55m

Pitch 1: 5.10a, 6 bolts, 2 bolt rap anchor ☆☆☆☆☆
Scramble up easy 5.4 climbing to a slab ledge with 1 bolt for the start. There are 2 bolts to the right which are for *Snowflake*. Begins at the waist high bolt and climbs direct to a 2 bolt anchor.
Pitch 2: 5.10a, 6 bolts, 2 bolt rap anchor ☆☆☆☆
Climb along the slab to an arete to the anchors on the left which it shares with *Tinsel Moose*. Can be climbed as one long pitch with a double rope rappel.
FA: Perry Solmonson, Carl Tobin

7 Snowflake 5.8 ☆☆☆☆☆ 41m

Gear to 1", 2 bolt rap anchor
Climb easy 5.4 slab with bulges to a ledge where there are 2 bolts for a belay anchor. This is a good place to start the climb. Follow the obvious large and hollow sounding flake on the right which goes all the way to the top. Bring lots of small cams with some medium cams and stoppers to fill in. There is a new anchor on top of the flake that eliminates the old finish, which was a traverse on the grass to the anchors of *Thin As Ice*. Rappel from the anchor on top of the flake to the belay bolts (34m) or back to the ground with double ropes (41m).

8 Gumby Drop 5.6 ☆☆☆☆ 29m

8 bolts, 2 bolt rap anchor
Start at the top of another scramble grass gully. Begin at the right of the slab and climb big chickenheads for 8 bolts staying right. Hook right after the last bolt to walk across loose dirt to a 2 bolt rap anchor.

9 Mr. Bill 5.9+ ☆☆☆ 22m

2 bolts, Gear to 1", 2 bolt anchor
Start in a very defined corner. The lower crack offers little for protection but there is plenty after leaving the corner. First bolt is just over the upper lip then one more bolt on a face crux before the anchors.
FA: David Whitelaw, Amy Johnson 1987

10 Possum Kingdom 5.10a ☆☆☆☆☆ 25m

1 bolt, Gear to 1", 2 bolt rap anchor
From *Mr. Bill* walk right around the corner to a little alcove just before a load of alders. Follow a lonely crack which curves to the right and make grunting sounds. Leave that crack and continue up a more vertical thin crack using chickenheads for support. There is 1 bolt near the bottom that was used on early ascents. Bring offsets for the best placements. The best way to describe this route would be, "spicy."
FA: Rik Derrick, Kip O'Kelly

11 Random Samples 5.9r ☆☆☆ 25m

4 bolts, Gear to 1", 2 bolt rap anchor
This excellent climb goes from horizontal to horizontal with gear in each. It climbs through really good chickenheads in between placements until the upper face, which is protected with bolts.
FA: David Whitelaw, Dave Freeman 06.29.1988

There are multiple approach paths to the next two routes. Both approaches have their difficulties. The original approach traversed from high in the left corner nearly even with the anchor. This is a slick and steep approach where a fall would have bad consequences. The newer path follows from the belay bolt of Unattainable Ease and heads straight toward the anchor using gear.

12 Media Man 5.8r ☆☆☆ 28m

4 bolts, 2 bolt rap anchor
Once on the face climb up left along a bolt line. Bring slings to use knobs as protection as there are not many bolts on this route. Rappel back to the belay anchor.
FA: David Whitelaw, Amy Johnson 07.02.1988

13 Still Shakey After All These Years 5.10a ☆☆☆☆ 28m

9 bolts, 2 bolt rap anchor
Same start as *Media Man*. From the two bolt belay anchor move right up the ramp and across the blank face to the second set of chickenheads. Climb directly through or just left of the bolt line for fun 5.10b slab climbing. Rappel back to the belay anchor.
FA: David Whitelaw, Scott Mignery 1990

Rene Welty during the FA of Rainbow Coalition

9
10
11
12
13
14
15
16

14 Unattainable Ease 5.8, 5.8, 5.6 ☆☆☆☆ 55m

This climb is located down and right of *Possum Kingdom*. Follow the same approach as *Possum Kingdom* by moving right from the main trail toward a steep short scramble to the base of the climbs. Then move right along the cliff edge for about 20m until you reach a single bolt with a large quicklink for the belay.

Pitch 1: 5.8, 2 bolts, Gear to .5", 1 piton, 2 bolt rap anchor ☆☆☆ 15m

This pitch often is a little wet at the start where the gear goes. Place a piece of gear or two and then pull up right toward the ledge. You can reach up on the ledge and clip the piton, if feeling funky. Then walk the ledge right for 2 bolts to an anchor on a nice ledge. Bring your gear here to rappel back to the ground or rappel from the top of pitch 2 back to the start of the climb with a 70m.

Pitch 2: 5.8, 8 bolts, 2 bolt rap anchor ☆☆☆☆½ 28m

This fully sport pitch is excellent fun through a river of chicken heads. Easy climbing leads to the crux (don't stray far from the bolts) and then to a final steep wall with big holds. The last few holds can occasionally be wet but the bolt will be at chest level and they are big holds. End on a large grassy ledge.

Pitch 3: 5.6, Gear to 3", 2 bolt rap anchor ☆☆☆½ 12m

If this was close to the ground it could be as popular as *The Slot* on the Monolith. It's enjoyable climbing with gear everywhere. Mostly medium to large sizes from .25 and up to 3". Although comfortable leaders could use a BD Camelot #2 and below.

Descent: Each anchor is beefy 1/2" SS bolts and a large ring for lower or rappel. This makes each rappel very pleasant. From the final anchor rappel or lower through the ring back to the ledge atop pitch 2. Then rappel to pitch 1 anchor. From here go straight down to the ground by rappelling over the top of *Stranded by a Stinger*. If you are lowering back to the original ledge and you have a 70m rope, then you can lower from the top of pitch 2 back to the start ledge and your gear. Tie knots in the end!

FA: Kelsey Gray, Kate Day, Dan Linnell, Ryan Senko 2019

Karin Dau climbs her way up Possom Kingdom. This is a surprisingly stout lead for many, what looks like a nice finger crack generally leads to somewhat flaring gear and climbing on the face. The small chickenheads help supplement the thin crack. Bring small gear, and offsets are also especially useful. It can also help to bring some tree trimmers or a small saw as the alder at the base of the route grows quickly. It was completely cut back in 2020 and will likely be obscuring the base of the route within a few years. (Courtesy John Borland)

15 Devil's Hooch 5.10d ☆☆☆ 12m

5 bolts, 2 bolt rap anchor

Climbs a short face of fun tricky moves. There are two ways to start, from the lower left into a short corner on darker rock before heading into the steep or move into the second bolt from the right on a higher ledge. Either way the crux comes up high with some good fall potential. More moves than you would expect from a short climb. Can also be led into the start of *Unattainable Ease* by continuing past the anchor to the belay bolt above.

FA: Kelsey Gray, Dan Linnell

16 Stranded by a Stinger 5.10b ☆☆☆☆ 17m

7 bolts, 2 bolt rap anchor

This route is located below *Unattainable Ease* and is directly in line with the rappel for that route when lowering off the first pitch anchor. An enjoyable climb with great climbing on unique holds. Start in a corner and move right to the first bolt. There is another bolt somewhat hidden above the large ledge. A good belayer is important moving from the 3rd bolt to the 4th but there is a great clipping hold to make the next clip. Excellent roof moves lead to the anchor. Bolted over several years with plenty of help cleaning and a bee sting to the face (bees have since moved on).

FA: Kelsey Gray, Wongi Kim, Kate Day, Michael Walker, Beatrice Williams 2020

Regan Marin climbing Snowflake with
Rachel Lowrance on belay.

The Broken Ones AM 65min

Approach:
Start at the trailhead for Reed Lakes and hike the main trail. Continue toward Reed Lakes at the Snowbird cutoff after about 1.5 miles from the parking lot. Cross several streams and stay low in the valley. There is a trail for the Beaver Dams and this is usually the best trail to take to get to the base of the wall. Stay low in the valley and boulder hop your way until you are in line with the crag. Head directly uphill toward the wall. It can be easy to miss this wall as it is higher above the valley than the surrounding walls.

Area:
The valley beyond Snowbird Slab holds a lot of hidden gems, and this is one of those routes that looked obvious when seen from the valley floor. This wall currently holds just one route. It splits the wall through the steep face and into the overhangs. It's a challenging climb with some enjoyable airy moves bolted by Kelsey Gray, Kate Day, and Ryan Senko in 2018. It is possible to access this climb from above by hiking to the top of the ridge and then straight down near a large clean boulder. Initially, it may not be easy to find the anchor but you shouldn't have to do any dangerous scrambling to access it. Avoid the top approach if it has recently rained, as the steep grass downhill can be very slippery when wet.

1 Broken Ones 5.12a ☆☆☆☆ 32m
8 bolts, 2 bolt rap anchor
Start on the easy slab and climb to the small wet roof. This section usually seeps at all times of the year. One big move will get you above the roof, move right to the flaring crack. Strenuous moves lead to a good undercling rest (if you can find it) before the crux. Move right through the thin crux to the jugs and ledge for a good rest. Awkward moves on to the slab and then head into the corner. Climb high right into the corner before moving left on the obvious jug. Pull around the corner and on to the left slab. Continue above the grass to the anchor. There are a few places on route where gear can fill in between the bolts, specifically after the crux bolt and the last bolt (gear to .5").

Noah Samuelson getting into the goods on Rise (p.161) at The High Dive. (Courtesy John Borland / morffed.com)

Devil's Gully 70min

Approach:

Start at the trailhead for Reed Lakes and hike the main trail. Continue toward Reed Lakes at the Snowbird cutoff after about 1.5 miles from the parking lot. Cross several streams and stay low in the valley. There is a trail for the Beaver Dams, and this is usually the best trail to take to get to the base of the wall. Stay low in the valley and boulder hop your way until you are in line with the crag. Head directly uphill toward the wall. This wall is smaller and can be easy to miss but it is just before the Inferno Wall.

Area:

This small area doesn't have a lot of routes but can be a fun spot for a group to get some easy climbing with low risk. The three short routes on the face can all be climbed from the same anchor and require low commitment. When I first thought about developing this area it was with another climber who was recently preparing to be a parent. We talked about how this crag would be a good option as it didn't seem much higher than a big highball boulder and it felt like it had low consequence. I think Alaskans may be unique in thinking that a high alpine crag over an hour from the car may be a good place to bring a newborn.

1 Beefy Ankers 5.8 ☆☆☆ **12m**
4 bolts, 2 bolt rap anchor
Start on easy ground following rails to the first high bolt. Continue to a small roof before the finish crux. Same anchor as the next two routes.
FA: Kelsey Gray, John Borland, Robert Suenram 2018

2 Baby Tuolumne 5.8 ☆☆☆ **11m**
2 bolts, Gear to .25", 2 bolt rap anchor
A thin crack that angles up toward bolts. Fun underclings at the crux.
FA: John Borland, Kelsey Gray, Robert Suenram 2018

3 Devil's Bush 5.9 ☆☆☆ **11m**
3 bolts, 2 bolt rap anchor
Easy climbing leads to a steeper face with the crux right at the lip. These climbs are enjoyable but short and would be higher stars if longer. Shares an anchor with the previous two climbs.
FA: Robert Suenram, Kelsey Gray, John Borland 2018

4 Fully Stocked 5.10a ☆☆☆½ **17m**
Gear to 2", 2 bolt anchor
Follow the arete on very small gear. Micros are helpful for the crux and gear can be hard to find if the cracks are grown in. Tricky placements at the crux may make this a scary lead for some. Continue the arete on easier ground to the anchor.
FA: Kelsey Gray, Naomi Stock 2018

5 New Age Petro 5.8 ☆☆☆ **15m**
5 bolts, 2 bolt anchor
This route is located on the right side of the crag and required a lot of cleaning away of devils club to put it in. Follow up the face using good holds to the top of the crag. Uses the same anchor as *Fully Stocked*.
FA: Kevin Goodman, Kelsey Gray 2018

Inferno Wall 75min

Approach:
Start at the trailhead for Reed Lakes and hike the main trail. Continue toward Reed Lakes at the Snowbird cutoff after about 1.5 miles from the parking lot. Cross several streams and stay low in the valley. There is a trail for the Beaver Dams, and this is usually the best trail to take to get to the base of the wall. Head directly toward the Inferno Wall staying low in the valley. If you miss any of these trails just start heading toward the Inferno Wall whenever you can. There is no definitive trail. Crossing on the right side of the boulder field is usually easier.

Area:
This area hasn't changed since the last book, but the original lines and newer routes still make it a highly enjoyable area. *Infernal Sunshine* is probably the longest all sport line in Hatcher Pass at 3 pitches. The cruxes are well protected and the climbing, as well as the view, is well worth a trip. *Collateral Damage* was put up in 2015, and at first was thought by a few to have been a retrobolt of *Escape From the Lemming Ranch*. After a long discussion online, which included the first ascensionists, it was decided that it was not a retrobolt. That being said, you can definitely traverse from the third bolt on *Collateral Damage* to the first gear placement of *Lemming Ranch*. Previous to the bolts on *Collateral Damage* this climb was rarely done as a fall before the first gear would have probably ended in grave injury or death. Making matters worse, I broke off the first gear placement block without much effort. This makes the climb even more of a runout. If you want to have the full original effect, then climb it direct from the one bolt anchor on the ledge and just hold on tight as the gear doesn't come for a while.

As of 2016 all anchors have been replaced with stainless steel bolts and rappel rings.

1 Infernal Sunshine 5.10a, 5.11c, 5.11b
☆☆☆☆ **66m**

Possibly the longest all sport line in Hatcher Pass. This whole route can be climbed and rappelled on a single 60m rope with 9 draws. There are possible gear placements but not necessary.

Pitch 1: 5.10a, 4 bolts, 2 bolt rap anchor *15m*

Climb the right side of the triangular lower wall starting on big ledges and continue left to exit the top of the triangle.

Pitch 2: 5.11c, 7 bolts, 2 bolt rap anchor *23m*

The crux comes right away on this stellar pitch with powerful moves and hidden holds. Once past the 4th bolt, move right to continue on chickenheads to the anchor above a small grass ledge.

Hatcher Exit Var.: Once past the 4th bolt, head direct on gear to 2" to meet with the same anchor.

Pitch 3: 5.11b, 9 bolts, 2 bolt rap anchor *28m*

Another fun crux through a roof to more steep chickenheads. Follow the bolts out left of a small roof at the top of the cliff and onto the grass ledge. Walkoff or rappel the route with a single 60m rope. Tie knots.

FA: Kelsey Gray, Kris Klien
FFA: Daniel Linnell

2 Collateral Damage 5.11c ☆☆☆ 28m

9 bolts, Gear to .25", 2 bolt anchor

The first bolt works as a belay bolt and a rappel bolt to get back to the ground. Scramble to the ledge and this climb exits the left side of the lower ledge. Climb two vertical dikes on bolts and move left to a small roof. The crux is at the roof. Finish over the grass, same anchor as the belay for the *Tax Man Taketh Away*.

FA: Kelsey Gray, Kris Klien 08.24.2015

Shasta Gray starting Escape from the Lemming Ranch.

3 Escape From the Lemming Ranch Var. 5.10b/r ☆☆☆ 29m

Gear to 2", 2 bolt rap anchor

Climb up to the large grass ledge and start on a very featured slab to the nice vertical crack. Climb this direct through to the finish. Move right for the anchor. Good holds although it is runout. Best as a toprope after having climbed *Escape From the Lemming Ranch.*

4 Escape From the Lemming Ranch 5.10b/r
☆☆☆☆☆ **29m**

Gear to 2", 2 bolt rap anchor

Scramble up to the grassy ledge and begin the climb on vertical dikes to a nice flaring crack. Move right into the corner system with a thin finger crack. Bring plenty of small cams or stoppers for this section. Also this pitch is notorious for zippers; place opposing pieces at the base of the dihedral. Move left at the roof through underclings to another crack and climb direct over the lip.

FA: Roger Pollard, Jim Sweeney 1987

5 The Tax Man Cometh 5.10a ☆☆☆☆ 30m

Gear to 2", 2 bolt rap anchor

Start on the far right section of the main wall before the corner that goes to a nasty chimney. This route is not located on the same ledge as *Escape From the Lemming Ranch*, although it does use the same anchor. Climb a short flake and then follow on cracks up and left. Continue to a large grass ledge and use the same anchor as *Escape From the Lemming Ranch.*

FA: Steve Garvey, Roger Pollard, Jim Sweeney 1988

6 The Tax Man Taketh Away 5.10a ☆☆☆ 25m

3 bolts, Gear to 2", 2 bolt rap anchor

This route can be reached two ways. Walk to the top of the cliff and rappel in from a somewhat hidden anchor or by first climbing any of the previous three routes. The belay anchor (2 bolts) is down and left of the main anchor. Move through a fun slightly traversing slab and then head directly to a roof corner above. Gear can be sparse but is in the right places. Bring a green C3 or comparable size to keep from being runout.

FA: Kelsey Gray, Kris Klien 08.24.2015

7 Dark Chimney 5.8 💣 32m

Gear to 3", Slings anchor

The large obvious chimney in the corner. "It's dark and it smells wet," sounds about right. Best plan of attack for an anchor is to sling some rocks and make your way to the anchors for *Escape From the Lemming Ranch*, or belay from the top off gear and slung rocks. Beware of the loose blocks at the top.

8 Not Again 5.9r **50m**

Gear to 3", Slings anchor

Climb up a short dihedral crack to a grass ledge. This portion is deceiving as it makes you think you are on a decent route. If you really want to have a good time, belay and rappel from here. If you are into something different move up left into another corner and pull onto the arete. Move out right along a broken ledge with loose rocks to a grass ramp. Climb up the grass ramp and look for large rocks to sling. By this time the rope drag makes you feel as though you're carrying your partner up. Bring slings for every piece and the anchor. Walkoff or double rope rappel.

FA: Kelsey Gray, John Borland 2008

9 Cow Parsnip Bastards 5.8 ☆☆ **45m**

Gear to 2", Slings anchor

Start on a very featured slab with small roofs. Pull over the roof on huge chickenheads and cracks. Move right over the top of the large roof until topping out. There are chickenheads to sling and some pro in the horizontal cracks.

FA: Jim Sweeney, Randy Zernzach 1987

The right side of the cliff, beyond Dark Chimney has several routes but no bolts or fixed gear. This section tends to be a "choose your own adventure" style of climbing where you'll sling chickenheads for protection and run it out from marginal protection. While there may not be a picture to show the routes, I'm not entirely convinced it would help if there was.

Pulp Culture Wall 80min

Approach:
Park at the trailhead for Reed Lakes. Walk the main trail to the cutoff for Snowbird and Reed Lakes. Continue on the trail toward Reed Lakes as it switchbacks up the hill past Snowbird Slab. Continue following the switchbacks up the hill and stay on the main trail until it starts to cross the river from the right to left. Stay on the right side of the valley and don't cross the river. Look for Pulp Culture Wall on your right and head straight for it. Pulp Culture Wall is around 2.75 miles from the parking lot.

Area:
The Pulp Culture Wall is characterized by chickenheads and long routes. The crag is in a beautiful setting and the routes are generally enjoyable. *Pulp Culture 5.8+* is one of the longest single pitch climbs included in this book, especially of such high quality. Outside of just a few pieces of necessary gear, it is essentially a sport climb. There are a few newer short routes on the wall, but the area has not seen much development. Most of the anchors and bolts have been replaced in this area as of 2016.

Ezra Samuelson on the excellent climb Pulp Culture. (Courtesy John Borland / morffed.com)

k 5.7 ☆☆☆ **18m**

ap anchor

two new routes on the wall to the left of *Wiener Dog Butts*. This is the farthest left route. Start climbing into a small pod and then follow the bolts as they arch slightly right. The third bolt can be hard to see from the ground or until you get to it but there are no large runouts.

FA: John Borland, Dave Arnett 07.18.2014

2 Tracer Route 5.8 ☆☆☆ **18m**

3 bolts, 2 bolt rap anchor

The first bolt for this route is about 4 meters high, so there's a runout but on easy climbing with large chickenheads. The first bolt was from a previous route that traversed back into *Wiener Dog Butts*. Continue direct to use the same anchor as *Paperback*.

FA: Kelsey Gray, Tracy Borland 07.18.2014

3 Wiener Dog Butts 5.7 / 5.8 ☆☆☆☆ **20m**

5 bolts, 2 bolt rap anchor

Located 4 meters left of *Black Dog*. Climb chickenheads up easily through bolts direct to a ledge before another vertical wall. The anchors are located on the ledge. (5.8)

Var. Short Butts: 5.7, 4 bolts, 2 bolt anchor ☆☆☆

3m to the left of the normal start for *Wiener Dog Butts*. Climb to the first bolt of *Tracer Route* then move right to meet with the third bolt of *Wiener Dog Butts*.

FA: David Whitelaw, Amy Johnson 1991

4 Black Dog 5.10a ☆☆☆ **45m**

5 bolts, Gear to 1", 2 bolt rap anchor

Climb chickenheads to just left of the roof using thin pro and slung chickenheads. Meander around the face with cracks to the topout. Walk across the grass for a 2 bolt anchor. Walkoff or do a long double rope rappel.

FA: David Whitelaw, Doug Munoz 1991

5 Bombay Deluxe 5.9 ☆☆☆ **45m**

Gear to 3", 2 bolt anchor

Climb a broken corner with vegetation in sections. Seems to use the cracks mainly for protection as going on the face makes the climb easier. Climb out right in the corner then move left at the top for the anchor. Walkoff or double rope rappel.

6 Pulp Culture 5.8+ ☆☆☆☆☆ **55m**

9 bolts, Gear to 2", 2 bolt rap anchor

Start on a belay bolt about waist high on a lower portion of rock. Move right along grassy ledges toward a wide crack that thins and angles right. Pro is needed at the crack. Continue along on bolts angled to the right. Bring slings for every bolt; even with them the rope drag is huge. Walk across the grass ledge for the anchor. A very long climb. Walkoff is recommended.

FA: David Whitelaw, Amy Johnson 1990

This wall is reminiscent of Dermatologist Dream, but is not as steep. This causes the routes to be more moderate. A great place to climb easier routes on a sunny day.

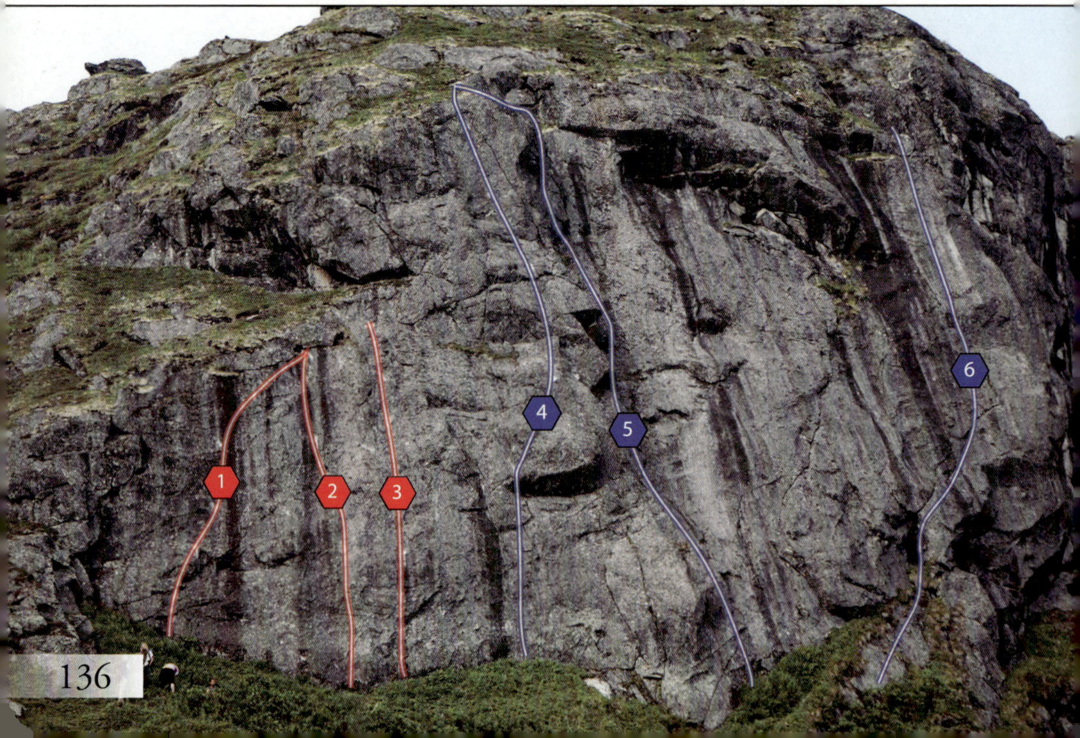

Noah Samuelson working King Ex (5.8) on Zydeco Wall (p.152)
(Courtesy John Borland / www.morffed.com)

Fatal Attraction Wall 90min

Approach:
Start at the trailhead for Reed Lakes and hike the main trail. Continue toward Reed Lakes at the Snowbird cutoff after about 1.5 miles from the parking lot. Cross several bridges over the streams and stay low in the valley. There is a trail for the Beaver Dams, and this is usually the best trail to take to get to the base of the wall. Head directly toward the Inferno Wall staying low in the valley. It is also possible to hike to the last few switchbacks up to Snowbird Slab and then continue along the base of the wall. The path through the bigger boulders here can take more time and makes route finding tricky. If you miss any of these trails, just start heading toward the Fatal Attraction Wall whenever you can. There is no definitive trail.

Area:
The Fatal Attraction Wall is the largest wall in the lower valley, but due to its location has seen little in the way of development. Thankfully, that is finally changing and it is starting to see new action. The original route on the wall is *Aerodogs*, a line that splits the middle face following a series of finger sized cracks. Recent years saw the addition of *Cantankerous Cranksters* and *Astroclam*. *Cantankerous Crankster's* first three pitches likely put it in contender for the longest stretch of sport climbing in Hatcher Pass. You'll never be disappointed with a trip into this area of the valley, as many new pitches combined with old classics make this a quality area. It is best as a middle to late season crag as water tends to run from the wall during the early season and *Aerodogs* rarely fully dries out.

Testing moves during the development of Cantankerous Cranksters. (Courtesy John Borland / morffed.com)

1 Cantankerous Cranksters 5.6, 5.7, 5.10c, 5.11a ☆☆☆☆☆ 115m

This climb is an excellent adventure of sport and trad, with safe climbing and bolted rap belays. The rating will intimidate plenty of climbers but the cruxes are all on bolts and even doing just the first 3 pitches is entirely worth it.

Pitch 1: 5.6, 6 bolts, 2 bolt rap anchor 35m

The first pitch is a long trek through several faces. Start on the easy slab and then cross the grass ledge to another face. Several more bolts will bring you to the next big grass ledge. This is also the start ledge for *Aerodogs.*

Pitch 2: 5.7, 4 bolts, 2 bolt rap anchor 18m

Go straight up from the belay on big holds and several bolts. There is a healthy distance between bolts but the climbing is easy and enjoyable. It is possible to combine this pitch and the next for one excellent pitch of 5.10 sport climbing.

Pitch 3: 5.10c, 8 bolts, 2 bolt rap anchor 25m

Move right from the anchor, the crux comes quickly and an additional bolt was added to protect this area. Avoid the sucker ledge out left after the crux and continue through a small roof move. More tricky climbing heads up to a relatively easy slab finish and the anchor on a nice grass ledge.

Pitch 4: 5.11a, 5 bolts, Gear to 3", 2 bolt rap anchor 37m

The final pitch adds a definite crux to the route. Head up to a bolt and get ready to pull on small, thin crimps. The shorter you are, the more difficult this section will be. Pull through the crux and left into a crack where a .75 or #1 BD cam works great. Follow the ramp to the right using two bolts and placing gear until you reach an enjoyable 5.7 crack. Follow this to the final 5.9 pull over a roof with the exposure of the whole route below you. Save some gear for the final pull over the roof as it can be tricky placements. The anchor is on a nice big ledge on the top of the cliff.

Descent: The unfortunate side of the final pitch is you will need to bring an 80m rope, two ropes, walkoff, or do a semi-dangerous downclimb. It is possible to downclimb from the grass ledge where a 70m rope reaches to get to the lower anchor. This is not ideal and it is best to bring two ropes for the rappel. There are plans to add an additional anchor above the current to allow for a single 70m to rappel. The rest of the route can be rappelled with a single 70m, stopping at each belay station on the way down. As always, tie knots in the end of your rope for every rappel.

FA: Kelsey Gray, John Borland 08.2017

2 Aerodogs 5.6 / 5.10b, 5.10c, 5.10 ☆☆☆ 110m

Standard rack, Gear anchors

I have very little information for this climb beyond the direction of climbing to the first anchor. The second pitch has had several exits although none of it gets climbed very often. It would be great to bring this climb back from obscurity with some cleaning but it often remains wet on the first pitch throughout much of the season. I am currently listing it here as historical reference and for anyone who wants to get the extra adventure. All information below is second hand; this route is for experienced parties only.

Pitch 1: 5.6 / 5.10b, Bolts, 2 bolt rap anchor 35m

The second pitch can be accessed multiple ways. There are two anchors on the grass ledge where the second pitch starts. The easiest access is to climb the first pitch of *Cantankerous Cranksters (5.6).* It is also possible to climb *Aerodogs (5.10b)* and then walk left along the edge to the base of the second pitch and start climbing. This pitch is the access pitch for the ledge.

Pitch 2: 5.10c, Standard rack, Piton + Gear anchor 45m

The second pitch is reportedly the best, being 150' finger crack with the crux at the end. Follow the right angling crack as it heads up toward the corner above.

Pitch 3: 5.10, Standard rack, Gear anchor 30m

There are cracks on the face above and it heads toward a large grass ledge. You can find a place to belay here or continue on the grass linking one long pitch to the top.

Descent: Walkoff the route, which would be more ideal than trying to rappel using the slings or old piton anchors. From the top, walk left to rappel *Cantankerous Cranksters* if you have two ropes, or walkoff the top of the cliff. If you plan to walkoff the top, then bring all your gear as the walkoff is easiest by coming down Reed Creek Trail.

FA: Steve Garvey, Jim Sweeney, Mark Yerkes 1988

3 Astroclam 5.10b ☆☆☆☆ 24m

5 bolts, One .4 BD cam, 2 bolt rap anchor

This pitch was installed as a variaton to the start of *Aerodogs*, which can also be started from the first pitch of *Cantankerous Cranksters.* Start below the overhang and pull on to the slab to clip a bolt, place the one piece of gear, and then pull the roof on a bolt. One big crux move here will get you on to the slab above. Follow more bolts to the large grass ledge with a bolted anchor below a small roof.

FA: Amos Swanson, John Giraldo 2017

1
2
3

Dermatologist Dream AM 70min

Approach:
Start at the Reed Lakes trailhead and walk the main trail to the two river crossings. The trail splits several times but you want to continue toward Reed Lakes and not the lower valleys. Continue on the main trail as it switchbacks over Snowbird Slab and follows right along the side of the mountain. There is no definite trail heading toward the Derma Wall, as it's normally called. Head down toward the wall from the main trail and cross the creek high on the boulders where it comes out of the rocks and your feet will stay dry. Continue on the grass and a rock gully to the main wall.

Area:
Dermatologist Dream is the black and white streaked wall on the left of the photo. The "Derma" wall is characterized by large chickenheads which cover nearly the entire face. This makes for quite the unique experience within the valley. There are other areas where chickenheads are present but they don't seem to have the same steep consistent nature. There is plenty of sun on these walls, much like the rest of the valley.

The anchors for climbs 1 - 5 were replaced in 2020 with stainless steel rap anchors. Cord should no longer be left on these anchors. There are several new routes as well on this wall that should help fill in some of the gaps and create an enjoyable cragging area. It is important to be delicate with the chickenheads on this wall as they can break and will erode over time. This is evident in climbs such as *Wild Kingdom,* which has become harder as the small features become smooth. A high quality crag that is not to be missed.

The excellent features of the Dermatologist Dream wall on display. Devin Kenley leads up Last Time to Selma with Marika Hintz on belay. (Courtesy Michael Hintz)

1 Fatal Flake 5.11a ☆☆☆ **23m**

1 piton, Gear to 2", 2 bolt rap anchor

Start in a vegetated corner and move into what quickly appears to be a crackless smooth feature. There is, or was, a pin here. Traverse left onto the face to get yourself some backup from chickenheads. Move right to the large detached, super sharp flake, and into a hand crack for the finish. Tiptoe on the blocks. Look for the anchor in the rock above a grass ledge. The old anchor was replaced in 2020.

FA: J.J. Brooks, Rik Derrick 1987

2 Wild Kingdom 5.12a ☆☆☆ **20m**

5 bolts, Gear to .25-.3", 2 bolt rap anchor

Pumpy moves, and the climbing seems to get harder as you go until the crux at the last bolt. There is decent fall potential on this climb so make sure to have a competent and attentive belayer. There is one place for gear that fits a small blue Metolius cam or gear in the .25 - .3" range. You will want this cam to eliminate a sizeable runout.

FA: J.J. Brooks

3 Huck A Turbo 5.10b ☆☆☆☆ 20m

3 bolts, Gear to 3", 2 bolt rap anchor

Climb large chickenheads to a small hand ledge at the first bolt. Enjoyable climbing leads to a corner with plenty of gear opportunities for small cams or stoppers. Continues along the corner pulling left and out for the anchor. Mostly small gear but there is one nice placement for a BD #3.

FA: Roger Pollard, Paul Wharton

The "Derma" wall is covered in chickenheads of all sizes but they can also be deceiving. Tread lightly, or they'll get smaller.

4 Last Time to Selma 5.10a ☆☆☆☆ 18m

6 bolts, One BD .4 cam, 2 bolt rap anchor

A new climb that follows a line of chickenheads up a dark streak. There is a crack between the third and fourth bolt that takes a BD .4 really well. Finish high on the upper face with a little more climbing to the anchor. Shares an anchor with *Bombs Over Tulsa.* Named after civil rights leader John Lewis and his last trip across the bridge over the Alabama River.

FA: Kelsey Gray, Regan Marin 07.31.2020

5 Bombs Over Tulsa 5.10b ☆☆☆☆ 18m

6 bolts, 2 bolt rap anchor

Starts on a good flake with the first bolt able to be clipped from the flake. The crux is at the start with it being easier the taller you are, but it is well protected. Continue on a straight line of bolts to high on the cliff. Named for the Tulsa Race Massacre on June 1, 1921.

FA: Kelsey Gray, Regan Marin 08.2020

6 Shish Kaknob 5.10a ☆☆☆☆ 14m

3 bolts, Gear to .5", 2 bolt rap anchor

Climb supremely large chickenheads for two bolts. Route then heads left to the 3rd bolt. Move up and right for the anchor; bring a nut tool to clean the gear placements as it tends to grow in.

FA: Grant Walker, Roger Pollard

7 Ontology 5.9+ ☆☆ 14m

3 bolts, Gear to .75", 2 bolt rap anchor

Located at the end of the grass ramp on the right side of the wall. Move just left of the roof and climb a bowl area. Finish left by pulling over the lip. Gear after the second bolt can help eliminate a possible runout.

FA: Paul Wharton

8 Fissure 5.7r ☆☆ 27m

Gear to 3", 2 bolt anchor

On the far right side of the main wall to the right of a large rock. Follow left in a wide crack to a ledge. Move right onto a flake and chickenheads. There is a bolt out right for *Dark Rhythm.* Continue left along the broken wide crack and finish out of a corner. Uses the same anchor as *Dark Rhythm.*

9 Dark Rhythm 5.10a/b ☆☆ 27m

2 bolts, Gear to 2", 2 bolt anchor

Scramble up the grass to a knobby face. Go direct over chickenheads with cracks intermittent for pro at the start. First bolt is high on the upper face with lots of little nubs for support. Once over the lip, look on the ground for the possibly covered anchor.

FA: Roger Pollard, Tom Evans

Birds of Prey AM 75min

Approach:
Start at the Reed Lakes trailhead and walk the main trail to the two river crossings at 1.5 miles in. The trail splits several times, but you want to continue toward Reed Lakes and not the lower valleys. Continue on the main trail as it switchbacks over Snowbird Slab and follows right along the side of the mountain. There is no definite trail heading toward the Derma Wall and Birds of Prey. Head down toward the wall from the main trail and cross the creek high on the boulders where it comes out of the rocks and your feet will stay dry. Take a right up the valley toward Birds of Prey, and as there is no trail, continue on the most obvious path off large boulders.

Area:
The Birds of Prey wall has been around for a long time but sees little traffic. One of the original routes on the wall *Birds of Prey* has even seen a few new bolts crop up because it had become so overgrown that someone thought they got a new first ascent. Either way it is a great route that will probably become a trade route as others realize just how enjoyable it is. The *Birdman Roof Project* is still unclimbed and is now an open project. The route called *The Jinx* was named Hashtag Crack in the previous guidebook as another group cleaned and climbed it much later. The cracks tend to grow back in. After receiving new information on the first ascent and names for the last four routes, that has now been updated.

1 Birdman Roof Project 5.? 30m
2 bolts, 1 piton, Gear to 3", 2 bolt anchor
Start by heading into several small corners and toward the steep roof crack. Hard steep jamming and liebacking will get you over the roof. Head right into another corner with some loose blocks. Mostly awkward moderate climbing with an intimidating crux.

2 Birds of Prey 5.10a ☆☆☆☆☆ 30m
3 bolts, Gear to 2", 2 bolt rap anchor
This awesome corner is a gem. Climb two bolts and then gear through fun corner climbing. The anchor is after the upper roof.
FA: Roger Pollard, Grant Walker

3 Brazilian Sex Wax 5.9 ☆☆☆ **28m**
9 bolts, 2 bolt rap anchor
Follow the arete with a high first bolt with some gear possible at the start. Bolts the rest of the way.
FA: Skine Boynton

4 The Jinx 5.9 ☆☆☆ **29m**
Gear to 3", 2 bolt rap anchor
A nice long moderate gear route. Follow a corner to a roof and then continue through a broken crack to the same anchor as *Brazilian Sex Wax*.
FA: Doug Munoz, Sandy Graham 1992

5 The Heretic 5.11a ☆☆☆ **20m**
5 bolts, Gear to 1", 2 bolt rap anchor
Start on some bulges with gear placements and climb toward the orange face with black streaks. Get ready to work to the top.
FA: Doug Munoz, Sandy Graham 1992

6 Curse 5.8 ☆☆☆ **23m**
Gear to 2", 2 bolt rap anchor
Follow ledges up and left to a crack that splits the upper orange face. Move right after the crack to the same anchor as *Witch Hunt*.
FA: Doug Munoz, Sandy Graham 1992

7 Witch Hunt 5.10b ☆☆☆ **23m**
2 bolts, Gear to 2", 2 bolt rap anchor
A fun beginner lead for the first half but the grade goes up at the bolts. Start on a series of fun cracks. Move left delicately on bolts to get to the anchor or step over the top after the crack and walk on the grass left to the anchor.
FA: Doug Munoz, Sandy Graham 1992

Dan Linnell testing his strength on Birdman Roof Project. (Courtesy John Borland / morffed.com)

Reed Creek Wall AM 65min

Approach:
Start at the trailhead for Reed Lakes and hike the main trail. Continue on the main trail which leads toward Reed Lakes at the Snowbird cutoff, after about 1.5 miles from the parking lot. Hike through the switchbacks up the corner and past Snowbird Slab. Continue along the mountain side staying high near the ridge. The valley will flatten for a little while between two rock sections before it curves left into Reed Valley. This is the first rock wall directly off the trail, with about a 10 second approach as you enter into this small valley.

Area:
This crag does not seem to get much traffic, even though it is the first wall in this specific area. Many of the climbs on the left side of the wall are good topropes and would be great for beginners, with easy to moderate routes and many variation possibilities. The area is spread out, and the last bulb of rock is the least desirable for climbs. In the Mark Hall topo, which has been circulated through the internet and in many printouts through the years, this wall is incorrectly labeled as the Dermatologist Dream wall. I then gave it the name of the Gap Wall during the first printing of this guidebook. After talking with David Whitelaw and a few others, I learned that they used to call it Reed Creek Wall. I decided to change it to reflect its history.

1 Mastercard 5.10a ☆☆☆ **12m**

4 bolts, 2 bolt rap anchor

Climb left of the large black streak. Move into a corner and right to the first bolt, which is pretty high up. Move left when the corner ends; enjoyable slab moves to the finish. Bring the sticky. Walk right up the grass to share an anchor with the next climb.

FA: David Whitelaw, John Mitchell

2 American Express 5.8 ☆☆ **14m**

1 bolt, Gear to 1", 2 bolt rap anchor

Climb the thick black streak on the left side of the wall to a finger side pull crack at the top. The only bolt is in the center of the route. Climb direct and walk over the grass a few meters to the anchor.

FA: David Whitelaw, Amy Johnson 1990

3 Karl Malden 5.8+ ☆☆ **14m**

2 bolts, Gear to 1", 2 bolt rap anchor

Climb or walk the grass to the ledge on top of the detached boulder. Climb a thin crack, which is lower and right of a corner above. Move into the corner and pull out right at the top for a bolt. Continue up and right to exit. Walk across the grass for the anchor.

FA: David Whitelaw, Amy Johnson 1990

4 Visa 5.9r ☆☆ **14m**

1 bolt, Gear to 2", 2 bolt rap anchor

Climb to the first bolt of the next climb and move left onto the face. There is pro, but it is badly spaced. I would recommend this route as a toprope since it is very easy to setup. Climb along on flakes staying left of the large black streak. Pull over the top and use the same anchor as the previous climb.

FA: David Whitelaw, Amy Johnson

5 Pickpocket 5.8 ☆☆☆ **20m**

2 bolts, Gear to 2", 2 bolt rap anchor

Start next to a detached boulder with a corner. Climb up from the corner to a small ledge with the first bolt just out of reach. Move right at the top for the anchor. A wet finish here may make this climb harder.

Var 2: Gear to 2", 2 bolt rap anchor

Climb the crack right next to the large roof. Move left at the pockets.

FA: David Whitelaw, Dave Freeman 1989

6 After the Gold Rush 5.10b ☆☆☆☆ 15m
5 bolts, 2 bolt rap anchor
A short climb and currently the only one on this section of the wall. Climb good-looking button head bolts to a new looking anchor. Move through crimpy holds up the white streak direct to the anchors.
FA: David Whitelaw, The Kid 1992

The next 3 climbs are located further right down the wall than the last climb, on a section of rock that resembles a large bulb. It seems to bulge off the wall oddly and has intermittent cracks for placements.

7 Alembic Flagon 5.11b ☆☆☆ 9m
Gear to .25", 2 bolt rap anchor
Climb in a small corner on the right side of the indented area. A fall in this spot could be painful, and the gear is thin. Climb through hard moves in this slightly overhanging section and pull onto cracks in the face. Continues direct. Move right to the anchors. Pro seems to runout after halfway on easier ground.

8 The Gourd 5.9 ☆☆ 9m
Gear to .25", 2 bolt rap anchor
Start high right and traverse to the left in the middle of the slab. Move direct from here to the anchors. Climbing direct from the lower section makes this harder (5.11a).

9 Orange Pickle 5.7 ☆☆ 9m
Gear to .25", 2 bolt rap anchor
Start high right on the slab and climb through blocky areas to a small corner. Continue up and left of the vegetation.

This small section of rock does not see much traffic. The routes are short and would probably produce the same amount of enjoyment from bouldering.

Zydeco Wall PM 65min

Approach:
Park at the trailhead for Reed Lakes. Walk the main trail to the cutoff for Snowbird and Reed Lakes. Continue on the trail toward Reed Lakes, as it switchbacks up the hill past Snowbird Slab. Continue following the switchbacks up the hill and stay on the main trail until it crosses the river from the right to left. You will go up a short steep section and be below Reed Creek Wall. Once at the gap, where the trail becomes flat for a short amount of time, the wall will be on the right. Zydeco Wall is around 2.5 miles from the parking lot.

The photo below is taken from the Reed Lakes Trail, which passes below the cliff. It is an easy boulder hop to the base of the cliff.

Area:
This is probably the least used area in the gap when it comes to developed routes. Most of the routes were cleaned in 2014, but they could still use increased traffic. These range from true slabs with almost no visible holds to excellent horizontals that seem to be right where you need them. The bolts are sparse but protect the cruxes well and the entire cliff was also rebolted in 2014. With traffic, these are some of the best slabs around; without they are doomed to fall back under the moss.

Beyond the enjoyment of the climbing, this area of the trail is one of the more beautiful spots. The river slows in this section of the valley creating beautiful blue waters that flow between boulders. As with the couple of travelers in the photo above, it is a great place to stop and spend a little extra time on your way up the valley.

1 Cajun Slave Girl 5.8 ☆☆ 30m

2 bolts, Gear to 1", 2 bolt rap anchor

Climbs directly toward the bolts using small intermediate cracks for thin gear. Depending on the amount of vegetation, it could feel runout.

FA: David Whitelaw, Marci Baker

Graywater Var. 5.9: Start high left on the slab and climb toward the right, crossing cracks at an angle toward the first bolt high on the face. Climb out right and up to a larger horizontal crack. Traverse far left along this crack until under another bolt. Move direct from here to the anchor.

FA: Kelsey Gray, Shasta Gray

2 Queen Ida 5.8 ☆☆ 31m

1 bolt, Gear to 1", 2 bolt rap anchor

This climb goes up the center of the slab and has seen some cleaning but will probably need more to make it a quality route. There is only one bolt on the route and the rest is gear. Finish on the same anchor as *Cajun Slave Girl.* Those new to slab climbing and cragging in Hatcher Pass will probably find these more scary and intimidating than the grade would lead them to believe.

FA: David Whitelaw, Amy Johnson

3 Zydeco Fool 5.10a ☆☆☆☆ 32m

1 bolt, Gear to 2", 2 bolt rap anchor

Start at the lowest section of the slab and climb along on some ledges toward a scoop in the wall below the crack. This is the first small crux and will require some small gear. Head left onto great horizontals that will show up right when you want them to, stay left of the larger crack. The topout is strangely difficult but is protected by a single bolt.

FA: David Whitelaw, John Trautwein

4 King Ex 5.8 ☆☆☆ 32m

Gear to 2", 2 bolt rap anchor

Climb the large crack on the right side of the wall. The pro can be tricky at the start but continue on and enjoy fun moves through the crack. You can exit over the top of the crack to use the same anchor as *Zydeco Fool* or move left and finish on the last bolted crux move of *Zydeco Fool (5.10a).*

FA: Kelsey Gray, Shasta Gray

Bring a nut tool to clean out placements. The white colored rock in the photo is from an extensive cleaning mission to try and bring this wall back from obscurity. It takes constant effort to keep the crevices clean and it can make a significant difference when everyone does their part.

The Barnyard AM 75min

Approach:
Start at the Reed Lakes trailhead and walk the main trail to the two river crossings before beginning the switchback trail up past Snowbird Slab. Continue on the main trail as it switchbacks over Snowbird Slab and continues right along the side of the mountain. Walk past Reed Creek Wall and Zydeco Wall. The Barnyard walls are the farthest down the gap before the trail rounds the corner left and heads toward Lower Reed Lake. There are no general trails to these climbs; pick your best way over the boulders and head to the base of the cliff. All of the anchors for the climbs on the Barnyard, with the exception of *Soul Man (5.10a)* and *Unknown #6 (5.10x)*, can be easily accessed by walking around the left of the block and taking a short scramble to the top.

Area:
The Barnyard is a great place to spend an afternoon overlooking the slow moving Reed Creek and beautiful valley setting. The valley flattens out in this area and allows the stream to slow and provide some great swimming opportunities for a hot day.

After talking with David Whitelaw, the name of The Barnyard was settled on. There are some great routes in this small area and a lot of possibility. *Soul Man (5.10a)* sits alone on a section of wall separated from the other climbs. This is the first climb that you will come to when approaching the crag and is well worth climbing. Between the two areas is a decent sized overhanging wall. There is recent rockfall evidence in some places but overall it looks generally solid and will probably see a few climbs.

The beautiful view from The Barnyard looking toward Outpost Peak.

The first section of The Barnyard only has one route, but it is very enjoyable. There is a great deal of rock all around, and I hope development comes to this area. When looking for this route, walk on the trail toward Lower Reed Lake and there is a large wall with overhanging roofs on the left. This wall is located before those roofs and after Reed Creek Wall.

1 Soul Man 5.10a ☆☆☆☆ **29m**

8 bolts, 1 piton, 3 bolt anchor

The only climb on this portion of the wall. A very enjoyable route. The first bolt is pretty high and on not so easy ground so be careful or risk flying down the hill. The climb begins on the whitest section of rock. Climb up to a fun undercling and lieback, then move left across the face to a ledge. Move left over the next bulge. It is a bit runout here on easy ground (5.6) and some S/M gear would help eliminate the runout.

FA: David Whitelaw, Steve Garvey

2 George Orwell 5.8+/r ☆☆

5 bolts, 2 bolt rap anchor

Climb the left side of the rock feature. Start on top of a pointed ledge below two bolts inches apart. Climb up and left onto a blocky baby roof and move direct from here. There is a bit of a runout after the last bolt that I used one green Metolius TCU to eliminate.

FA: David Whitelaw, Greg Bombeck

3 Monocle 5.8 ☆☆

Gear to 4", 2 bolt anchor

Climb the obvious large crack just left of the arete. Follow the crack until it meets with the start of *George Orwell*. Climb a few meters for a two bolt anchor or sling the horn; by this time you're pretty much already on the ground and ready to start the previous route.

4 Political Satire 5.9, 5.7 ☆☆☆

Pitch 1: 5.9, 1 bolt, 1 piton, S/M Gear, 2 bolt anchor

Climb the start of *The Pig* and move left at the center of the wall on a nice ledge all the way to the arete where there is a 2 bolt belay anchor.

Pitch 2: 5.7, 4 bolts, 2 bolt rap anchor

Climb from the belay keeping left near the arete. Climb direct to share anchors with *George Orwell*, which are over the lip. Both pitches could be linked, but the rope drag would be tremendous.

FA: David Whitelaw, Greg Bombeck 1992

Most of the rock is good quality, although usually covered in a layer of lichen. I had heard of a project that went up the steep section of the face and connected with Political Satire; last reports put it in the 5.12 range. The updated information for Unknown 5.10x route has once again missed its way into this book. Climb at your own risk.

5 The Pig 5.9 ☆☆☆

3 bolts, 1 piton, Gear to 2", 2 bolt anchor

Climb right up the vegetated ramp and move up on loose blocks. Move left out of the blocks to the first bolt and continue left to a nice ledge. Continue its leftward trend to a flake. Pull over the flake and right along a crack to the anchor.

FA: David Whitelaw, Amy Johnson 1992

6 Unknown 5.10x

2 bolts, Unknown anchor

Behind The Barnyard, this climb is previously rated at 5.10x. Climb up into a corner and climb direct into the overhang. Move on gear to the finish. Probably has the x rating because of the length to the first bolt which looks unprotectable. Climb at your own risk. I did not climb this route so I do not know the status of it.

UPPER REED VALLEY

	CRAG	SUN & HIKE	ROUTES	RANGE	PAGE
1	Monkey Face	☀ 🏃100min	7	5.8-5.11c	158
2	The High Dive	☀ 🏃100min	8	5.7-5.11c	160

There are several other crags in this area, as well as some larger routes up the surrounding peaks. There is plenty to explore. Start at the Reed Lakes trailhead and walk the main trail to the Snowbird cutoff. Continue on the main trail to the right as it crosses several streams over nice bridges and switchbacks over Snowbird Slab, to continue toward the pass along the side of the mountain. Walk past the Reed Creek Wall and Zydeco Wall. Continue to follow the well-worn trail left around the bend and toward Lower Reed Lake. The trail will lead to the pass where it begins to round right toward Upper Reed Lake, and the cliffs are immediately on the right.

Monkey Face 100min

Approach:
Start at the Reed Lakes trailhead and walk the main trail to the Snowbird cutoff. Continue on the main trail to the right as it crosses several streams over nice bridges and switchbacks over Snowbird Slab, to continue toward the pass along the side of the mountain. Walk past the Reed Creek Wall and Zydeco Wall. Continue to follow the well-worn trail left around the bend and toward Lower Reed Lake. The trail will lead to the pass after Lower Reed Lake where it begins to round right toward Upper Reed Lake, and the cliffs are immediately on the right.

(Courtesy John Borland / www.morffed.com)

Area:
Framed beautifully by Outpost Peak, Lower Reed Lake, and the surrounding valley, this area deserves some attention. Excellent for a day of cragging, there are plenty of solid anchors and fun routes to climb. The lake has many great camping areas and is a beautiful shade of blue. Most of the routes have easy access to the anchors from the top and good walkoffs. There is very little loose rock on the routes. If you get tired of climbing on this crag, which is hard to believe, then move to the small buttress of rock on the right. It is called Underdog Rock and there are a few routes that ascend this nice block.

In the previous guides, all of these climbs were listed as Unknown, but that has changed for several of the routes. Todd Fisher finished several of his long standing projects, and now three of the routes have additonal bolts and names. These climbs, which were already high quality routes, are now more accessible due to the additional hardware. Many of these routes are pushing 30m, so you should always tie knots in the end of your rope when lowering or rappeling. They may be longer or shorter depending on where you stand or how you clip.

1 Unknown 5.11 32m
Toprope, 2 bolt anchor
Climbs to the left of the arete up the face section with several horizontal cracks.

2 Unknown 5.11c ☆☆ 30m
Toprope, 2 bolt anchor
The last climb before the large left facing corner. Climb staying just right of the corner through sustained and pumpy ground. Uses the same anchor as the next climb. Plenty of loose rock.

3 Unknown 5.10c ☆☆☆ 30m
Toprope, 2 bolt anchor
Climb the black streak to the left most edge of the roof system. Continue direct over another roof to share an anchor with *Unknown #2.*

4 Mauled by a Marmot 5.10b ☆☆☆☆☆ 30m
8 bolts, Gear to 1", 2 bolt anchor
This line was recently finished and now has new bolts. Ascends the white streak up a featured face to multiple roofs. Move right at the top for the anchor. Shares an anchor with *Black Magic.*
FA: Todd Fisher

5 Black Magic 5.10c ☆☆☆☆ 30m
9 bolts, Gear to .5", 2 bolt anchor
Start low on the face and climb direct on bolts through several small roofs with the crux. This route used to be a dangerous runout to the top, but thankfully was finished and is now an enjoyable lead to the same anchor as *Mauled by a Marmot.*
FA: Todd Fisher

6 My 4-Legged Vulture 5.10a ☆☆☆ 29m
6 bolts, Gear to 2", 2 bolt rap anchor
Recently finished to be a safer lead. Start in a wide crack on the right side of the face and climb to a roof with good underclings. Go over the roof before the black streak and continue direct. Move immediately right at the grass to a good belay. Some gear can be used to eliminate short runouts.
FA: Todd Fisher

7 Unknown 5.8 ☆☆☆ 27m
Gear to 1", 2 bolt anchor
Begin just right of the left angling roof and climb direct on large holds, stays approximately 2 meters right of *My 4-Legged Vulture* and leads to the right side of the grass.

The High Dive 100min

Approach:

These cliffs are located at the far end of Lower Reed Lake. Start at the Reed Lakes trailhead and walk the main trail to the Snowbird cutoff. Continue on the main trail to the right as it crosses several streams over nice bridges and switchbacks over Snowbird Slab, to continue toward the pass along the side of the mountain. Walk past the Reed Creek Wall and Zydeco Wall. Continue to follow the well-worn trail left around the bend and toward Lower Reed Lake. The trail will lead to the pass where it begins to round right toward Upper Reed Lake, and the cliffs are immediately on the right.

Area:

This area is characterized by a huge roof system in the middle of the wall. There is one route that was completed to the base of the roof, but it seems unlikely that anyone has climbed clean all the way through. The reality of this area is that it likely won't be as popular as many of the other crags in this book, but that doesn't mean it's any lower quality. In reality, it is a crag with excellent routes. *Rise (5.9)* is the original multipitch route on this wall and is now joined by other high quality lines put up in the last few years by Todd Fisher and crew. It was obvious by anyone who spent time in this area that there was a lot of potential to the right of the High Dive Roof. This area is now being developed with new great multipitch lines such as *Killing Aphrodite (5.10d), Double (D)ihedral (5.10c)*, and single pitch routes at the base. This area is charactarized by high quality clean stone with abundant features. You will definitely have plenty to climb on a long day trip or even a weekend outing to Reed Lakes.

1 Wankers Away 5.8 ☆☆ **16m**
Gear to 2", Gear and sling anchor
Climb a small face left of the start for *Rise*. Follow a right trending crack using small gear. Use gear for the anchor and a slung block.
FA: Lang Van Dommelen, Chris Williams, Summer Holt

2 Rise 5.7, 5.6, 5.9, 5.6 ☆☆☆☆☆ **100m**
Although this climb can be done on gear to 3", the 4" cams are nice to have on this route.
Pitch 1: 5.7, Gear to 4", 2 bolt anchor *30m*
Climb the right leaning ramp with a corner through several steps to a large detached block. Be wary of loose flakes.
Pitch 2: 5.6, Gear to 2", 2 bolt rap anchor *30m*
Traverse right along the corner to the base of two cracks going up a vertical wall. A new 2 bolt rap anchor has been installed. It is possible to rappel from here straight to the ground using two 60m ropes.
Pitch 3: 5.9, Gear to 4", 2 bolt anchor *30m*
This pitch is the reason for climbing the other two pitches. Follow double cracks with excellent jams until the left crack ends. Follow right along the remaining crack until topping out under a large roof.
Pitch 4: 5.6, Gear to 2", 2 bolt anchor *10m*
Move out left of the roof and continue on a short pitch to a bolted anchor.
FA: John Borland, Tracy Borland, Kelsey Gray, Dane Ketner 08.20.2009

3 Killing Aphrodite 5.10b, 5.10d ☆☆☆☆☆76m
Pitch 1: 5.10b, 6 bolts, Gear to 2",
2 bolt rap anchor ☆☆☆☆☆ *50m*
The first bolt is high above a small rock face at the ledge. Gear to 2" can be used to reach the first bolt. Head straight up 4 more bolts and then continue direct to exit through the roof on excellent climbing using smaller gear. Put in gear right when exiting the roof at a good stance, the next bolt is high and hard to see, but the climbing is easy and straightforward. Two more bolts after the roof lead to the anchor on the face. The first pitch of this climb is long: bring plenty of gear.
Pitch 2: 5.10d, 2 bolts, Gear to 2",
2 bolt rap anchor ☆☆☆ *26m*
Head right to arete and some gear placements. There are two options here: hook left to the bolts and a hard move (5.10d) or continue up the right corner on some gear and bypass the bolts (5.7). Move left above the bolts to continue on the crack to the top of the cliff.
Descent: It is possible to rappel this route using a single rope but it takes care to do so. Rap diagonally to the right, to the anchors on top of P1 of *Double D(ihedral)*, then to *Sprinklers Save Lives*, then to the ground. Otherwise, two 60m ropes are needed to rappel the route.
FA: Todd Fisher, John Giraldo 2017

5
3
4
6
7
8

4 Sprinklers Save Lives 5.10c ☆☆☆ 21m

4 bolts, Gear to .4", 2 bolt rap anchor

This short route follows on excellent stone with the first bolt in white rock. Gear between the first and second bolt (a BD X4 .4 and .3 work great) then more bolts direct to the anchor on a ledge.

FA: Mat Brunton

5 Double D(ihedral) 5.10c, 5.10a ☆☆☆☆ 75m

Pitch 1: 5.10c, 6 bolts, Gear to 3", 2 bolt rap anchor ☆☆☆☆ *50m*

Originally this pitch started the same as *Killing Aphrodite* and then hooked right on an A0 move. The start has been moved to leave from the anchor of *Sprinklers Save Lives*, hooking left to meet with a thin crack that takes gear up to two bolts before the dihedral. Bring plenty of gear around the .75" to 1" range. Belay from the top of the dihedral. 50m from the ground or 30m from the *Sprinklers Save Lives* anchor.

Pitch 2: 5.10a, 2 bolts, Gear to 3", 2 bolt rap anchor ☆☆☆½ *25m*

Move right to go into the next dihedral. This one is trickier than the first but still enjoyable. Bring mostly smaller gear. From the top of the dihedral go direct on bolts, then easy climbing leads to the anchor on a large ledge.

Descent: Rappel back to the top of pitch 1 and then to the anchor of *Sprinklers Save Lives*. One more rappel will get you back to the ground. It may be possible to rappel to the ground from the top using the full stretch of two 70m ropes; tie knots in the end.

FA: Todd Fisher, Mat Brunton

6 2 Left Shoes 5.11c ☆☆☆ 21m

7 bolts, 2 bolt rap anchor

Starts right of *Sprinklers Saves Lives* and has some stout, well bolted, climbing. Use the same last bolt and anchor as *Sprinklers Save Lives*. Looks easier than it is.

FA: Todd Fisher

7 Coitus Interruptus 5.9 ☆☆☆☆ 20m

5 bolts, 2 bolt rap anchor

Follow clean granite features on the slab with dikes and chickenheads to an anchor below the next face.

FA: Christina, Andy Hoyt

8 Choke the Chicken 5.7 ☆☆ 20m

Gear to 2", 2 bolt rap anchor

Climb flakes to the right of *Coitus Interruptus* on the same formation. Follow on gear before hooking left to the anchor.

FA: Christina, Andy Hoyt

Lower Reed Lake is a beautiful tourquise colored lake that sits below Outpost Peak. The hike to this area is popular with good reason, and you'll often see campers setting up their tents at the toe of the lake. In addition to the areas included in this guide, there are several other cliffs with development nearby. Probably the largest unpublished (in this guide) is the Mile High Wall. This wall is high on the hillside and an additional 30 minute hike away on the south-east face of Lower Spire. It offers incredible climbing on an intimidating face. There are several places to find online documentation if you wish to visit this currently-in-development area. Numerous other cliffs abound above the lake and on the surrounding mountain sides, and exploration will often be rewarded with adventure.

INDEPENDENCE MINE AREA

	CRAG	SUN & HIKE	ROUTES	RANGE	PAGE
1	Independence Crag	Sun, 40min	10	5.9-5.11a	166
2	Ramparts Wall	AM, 50min	11	5.9-5.10d	171
3	The Mine Crag	Sun, 45min	18	5.7-5.11a	176
4	Renaissance Wall	AM, 60min	11	5.8-5.11+	180
5	Moai Wall	PM, 40min	5	5.5r-5.10a	183

Independence Mine Area has a few parking restrictions that are good to know about. It is off Hatcher Pass Road and is the only Hatcher Pass area in this book that cannot be reached by Archangel Road. Continue on Hatcher Pass Road past the hairpin turn and head uphill past Archangel Road. Continue on the paved road as it winds around toward Summit Lake. Take a right on North Gold Cord Road; this heads to Independence Mine. If it is early or late in the season, the upper parking area may be closed. If it is closed, then you will need to park in the lower area and walk the rest of the road adding another 15 minutes to hike times. If the gate is open then proceed to the upper parking area. It will cost $5 to park anywhere at or beyond the first gate, and it is important to make sure you leave before the gate closes or else you will have an angry park host threatening to lock in your car. In 2020 the gates closed at 7pm, considered too early by many.

Independence Crag

40min

Approach:
Independence Mine is off Hatcher Pass Road and is the only Hatcher Pass area in this book that cannot be reached by Archangel Road. Continue on Hatcher Pass Road past the parking area for Gold Mint Trailhead, and head uphill past Archangel Road. Continue on the paved road as it winds around toward Summit Lake. Take a right on North Gold Cord Road; this heads to Independence Mine. If it is early or late in the season, the upper parking area may be closed. If it is closed then you will need to park in the lower area and walk the rest of the road. If the gate is open then proceed to the upper parking area. It will cost $5 to park anywhere at or beyond the first gate. From the parking lot head up and left toward the water tunnel and most of the buildings. Follow a paved trail that heads to the old rail line and the water tunnel. Take the walkway until the water tunnel entrance. There should be a gap in the railing that leads to a dirt path and a sign that says Mill Loop Trail. Directly up and left, you should see Independence Crag. Follow the dirt path as it heads up valley. Continue taking well-worn trails to the left. Stay on the right side of the river until you are nearly parallel with the large dirt piles on the left. Cross the river and follow the thin trail over the top of the large mine debris. Continue along the wall to the base.

Area:
This is an excellent wall with almost every route being high quality. Most of the routes were put up by Pat Rinehart and Jason Moncrieff. They worked on these routes for years, and now we can all reap the rewards. The only route at the crag not put up by Pat and Jason is *Ivan the Impaler (5.11a)*. A fun line with a tiring crux on thin gear. This crag has a lot of great routes around the 5.10 range. Almost all the anchors have rings already on the hangers making it quick to go from route to route. With one of the best belay ledges in Hatcher, this is an easy place to spend the day.

1 23 Karat 5.10c/d ☆☆☆
16 bolts, Gear to 2", 2 bolt anchor
Same start as *24 Karat*, moves left of the first bolt and follows the very clean arete through super thin moves. After the 7th bolt you can move right to meet with *24 Karat*, or continue the route direct through several more bolts and some gear.
FA: Pat Rinehart, Jason Moncrieff

2 24 Karat 5.10b ☆☆☆☆
15 bolts, 2 bolt anchor
Start high on the cliff left of the main climbing area. Move immediately right over a roof and into a corner. Follow the bolt line with a hard crux at the top.
FA: Jason Moncrieff, Pat Rinehart

3 Project: Steeptitude 5.11+
Bolts, Gear, No anchor
Currently unfinished. Located on steep ground between the two sections that have routes. Hard crux.
FA: Jason Moncrieff, Pat Rinehart

4 Repelled by Steepness 5.10b ☆☆
Gear to 1", No anchor
This is a short crack (5m) that leads to a large corner with loose blocks. It was meant to continue through the upper roof, which proved to be very difficult and is without a line at the moment. Walkoff to the left.
FA: Jason Moncrieff, Pat Rinehart

5 TBD 5.10c ☆☆☆☆ **28m**
4 bolts, 1 piton, Gear to .25", 2 bolt rap anchor
Start in a deep corner and climb a steep blocky roof with a crack. Continue direct on easier ground with bolts and gear mixed.
FA: Pat Rinehart, Jason Moncrieff

6 999 5.10b ☆☆☆ **29m**
7 bolts, Gear to .25", 2 bolt rap anchor
Starts just right of the large corner and stays consistently about 2 meters from the left edge.
FA: Jason Moncrieff, Pat Rinehart 09.09.2009

7 Harvest Mode 5.10c ☆☆☆☆½ **31m**
8 bolts, 2 bolt rap anchor
Start under a piece of wood hanging from the wall. Several different variations to the start and all are about the same difficulty. After a few bolts move right and traverse the face, which gets progressively more difficult. After the last bolt go right on a slight runout to use the *Ivan the Impaler* anchor. It is also possible to go the anchor for *999*. The first bolt is 5 meters up.
FA: Pat Rinehart, Jason Moncrieff

8 Ivan the Impaler 5.11a ☆☆☆☆ 30m
4 bolts, Gear to 1", 2 bolt rap anchor
Begin on the ledge and climb into the overhang. Follow to a fun finger crack and into the crux. Once you're good and tired, climb a long section of 5.10 to the anchor.
FA: Chris Williams, Lang Van Dommelen

9 Avoid the Noid 5.10a ☆☆☆☆ 28m
9 bolts, Gear to 3", 2 bolt rap anchor
Start between two corners on a drill pocket. Hard start to the first bolt and continue through double roofs on excellent holds. Watch out for the giant block attached with wire. Avoid the impaler.
FA: Pat Rinehart, Jason Moncrieff

10 Slabbyville 5.9 ☆☆☆☆ 27m
10 bolts, 2 bolt rap anchor
Climb slab and a corner to a small roof. Move right into another dihedral then pull over the top. Possible gear between the third and fourth bolt.
FA: Jason Moncrieff, Pat Rinehart

Pat Rinehart developing another fine route with Jason Moncrieff on belay.

David Whitelaw

David Whitelaw began his climbing career at Leysin American School in Switzerland. With numerous weekend outings to Chamonix and the Bernese Oberland, David was firmly committed to the sport by the time he'd returned home to Seattle in 1973.

Thirteen years, two guidebooks, and many first-ascents later, David arrived in Anchorage as an illustrator/graphic designer and soon found himself married and the owner of a small design firm, not far from AMH.

It didn't take long before winter weekends in Eklutna had introduced him to friends like Roger Pollard, Tom Evans, Steve Garvey, and others. Roger was the one who actually made the connections introducing David to Paul Denkewalter and Andy Embick, and in doing so, laid the groundwork for several of the guidebooks that followed.

David bought his first Macintosh in 1988, and three weeks later, the first Hatcher Pass guide, *First Steps* went off to press. The computer design business was good, and it wasn't much longer before Embick's *Blue Ice & Black Gold* Valdez guidebook was in the works. A short year later, David, Roger Pollard, and Steve Davis had joined forces on the *Fat City & Urban Ice* ice-climbing guide. He also designed and produced the annual calendars for Alaska Mountaineering and Hiking for a little over ten years.

During his time in Alaska, he was responsible for many new routes in Hatcher Pass and along the Seward Highway. David also completed *Thin White Line*, the Seward Highway guide, just a few months before leaving Alaska in 1992. The tagline for that book is "87 not-so classic climbs on the Seward Highway."

Currently David resides in West Seattle, Washington.

Ben Olwell climbing Shelter in Place (p.175) at the Ramparts Wall, with Eric Roberts in the cave belay.

Ramparts Wall AM 50min

Approach:

Follow a paved trail that heads to the old rail line and the water tunnel. Take the walkway until the water tunnel entrance. There should be a gap in the railing that leads to a dirt path and a sign that says Mill Loop Trail. Directly up and left you should see Ramparts Wall. Follow the dirt path as it heads up valley. Continue taking well-worn trails to the left. Stay on the right side of the river until you are nearly parallel with the large dirt piles on the left. Cross the river and follow the thin trail over the top of the large mine debris. Continue along the wall to the base of Independence Crag. Horizontal hiking from here will bring you to the base of Ramparts Wall after another 5-10 minutes. During the early season the snow covers most of the boulders and it can be quicker to head straight to the crag on the snow; however, the boulders can produce big gaps that become crevasses. Be weary of hiking through the big boulder field when the snow cover is low. It is a 1.5 mile approach to the base of the crag.

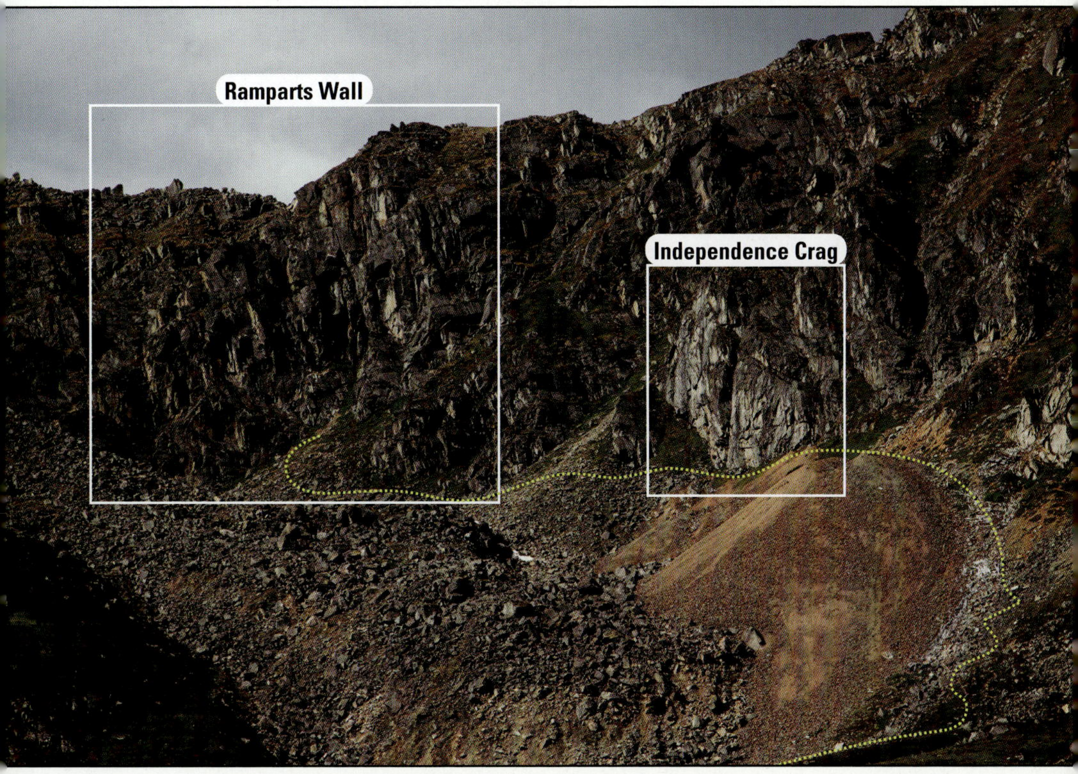

Area:

This new wall went overlooked for years, but it was just waiting for someone to put in the right amount of work. It has more of an adventure feel than the Independence Crag and is better for experienced parties than for mellow cragging. The intensive cleaning effort exposed thin cracks which often take small stoppers or TCU's and offer delicate movements on fun climbing. The area is still under development so care should be taken when venturing on to new unlisted routes and, as with most new cliffs, extra diligence should be taken to avoid knocking down any loose blocks.

Diggin It (5.10b) and *Get Your Ass to the Pass (5.10b)* are some of the best lines at the crag, and a real gem is *The Big Eddie (5.10c)*, a great route with enjoyable crack climbing that would be a highway if the approach was shorter. It is a great place to spend the day in the morning before moving to Independence Crag in the afternoon after the sun leaves the wall.

6
8
7
9
5
3
4
2
1

10
11
10

1 Dead Marmot 5.9 ☆☆ **24m**
7 bolts, Gear to 2", 2 bolt anchor
Move through a few bolts on a slab left of the steep orange face. Some gear between bolts help. Continue through a corner, then hook left around the arete to climb the left side. Traverse right at the top to the anchor. It's best thought of as an access pitch for *Corona Cracks*.
FA: Jason Moncrieff, Pat Rinehart

2 Necessary Evil 5.10c ☆☆☆½ **15m**
Gear to 1", 2 bolt rap anchor
Fun crack climbing with small finger jams and plenty of sidepulling. The arete to the right can help make it easier for some moves.
FA: Pat Rinehart, Jason Moncrieff 2020

3 Corona Crack 5.9 ☆☆☆ **24m**
Gear to 3", 2 bolt rap anchor, 2 bolt rap belay anchor
A series of cracks above *Necessary Evil*. Start at the ramp below *Rampart Rampage* and scramble/ solo to the belay anchor at the base: this can feel much more dangerous when wet. It is also possible to reach the belay anchor by climbing *Necessary Evil* and continuing on a grass scramble to the anchor or climb *Dead Marmot* and do a traverse pitch (5.4) to the belay. Move left of the belay, while staying out of the dirty corner, and pull over the block on big holds. Choose your crack and head up. After the first series of cracks there is another ledge and more corner or face climbing will get you to the anchor. Rappel from here to the belay anchor, then back to the ground.
FA: Jason Moncrieff, Pat Rinehart

Kate Day rounding the corner on the second pitch of Shelter in Place, an airy traverse that meets with Diggin It.

4 Rampart Rampage 5.10b, 5.6, 5.10b ☆☆☆½ **70m**
Pitch 1: 5.10b, Gear to 3", 2 bolt rap anchor *30m*
Small gear, stoppers, work best on this pitch, and on this climb in general. Start on the right of a slab and work your way left to the base of the first pitch. This pitch has plenty of grass and some blocks at the start but then leads into a fun crux over a small bulge on a finger crack. There is a traverse right at the crux that can be used as a bypass (5.9).
Pitch 2: 5.6, Gear to 3", 2 bolt rap anchor *18m*
More small gear tends to help on this pitch. Climb the corner on blocks that are loosening over time as the dirt behind washes away, although it's getting cleaner. At the top of the corner move right to exit instead of going straight through the moss.
Pitch 3: 5.10b, Gear to 2", 2 bolt rap anchor *20m*
The last crux on the route tends to be the mental crux as well. There are gear placements (TCU's or small nuts tend to work well) and you'll probably feel better placing a few of them. Interesting climbing on this pitch with the route's only protection bolt.
Descent: It is recommended that you rappel the route back to the ground using each rap station to make sure the rope doesn't get stuck. Three raps with a 60m rope will get you to the ground.
FA: Jason Moncrieff, Pat Rinehart 2016

5 Get Your Ass to the Pass (GYATTP) 5.9 / 5.10b, 5.10b ☆☆☆☆ **55m**
Pitch 1: 5.10b, 4 bolts, Gear to 2", mostly small gear, 2 bolt rap anchor *30m*
The first pitch starts high on grass ledge. Scramble up the gully and then traverse left to a 2 bolt belay anchor. You can also rappel from this anchor back to the ground. From the anchor, start in the left gully and follow a horizontal crack on to the face. Finding this crack seems to be the crux for some groups; it's important to climb high enough in the gully that you get to place gear in the crack before the right traverse. Clip the bolt and head direct to the base of the roof; two variations here to choose.
Var.1 5.10b: Move right following a horizontal crack under the roof to exit; three more bolts and gear will lead you to the anchor after the roof.
Var.2 5.9: Head left of the roof entirely on gear.
Pitch 2: 5.10b, 1 bolt, Gear to 2", mostly small gear, 2 bolt rap anchor *25m*
Start left of the anchor and follow thin cracks into the corner. Once out of the corner traverse right using a bolt to the next series of cracks. Rappel the route; a single 60m works. Tie knots in the end of your rope.
FA: Pat Rinehart, Jason Moncrieff

The next four routes are located above *GYATTP* and are accessed by climbing *GYATTP* to the top of the first pitch and traversing left. Descend using the *GYATTP* anchors.

6 Slabby 5.9 ☆☆☆ 20m

3 bolts, Gear to 4", 2 bolt rap anchor
Use gear at the base of the crack as a belay anchor. Traverse bolts left to the corner. Easy climbing from there leads to the top. Some loose material, although more solid than it originally looks.
FA: Jason Moncrieff, Pat Rinehart

7 The Snowshoes of Eddie Phay 5.10a ☆☆☆½ 20m

Gear to 2.5", 2 bolt rap anchor
Small gear is best for this climb. Interesting climbing in the corner to some protected face climbing.
FA: Jason Moncrieff, Pat Rinehart

8 EP2 5.10d ☆☆☆ 20m

Gear to 2", 2 bolt rap anchor
Small gear and TCU's are especially helpful on this pitch. Climb left toward *The Snowshoes of Eddie Phay* in the corner, but then move right at a thin crack. Hard liebacking on thin holds make this one spicy.
FA: Pat Rinehart, Jason Moncrieff

9 The Big Eddie 5.10c ☆☆☆☆☆ 21m

Gear to 3", 2 bolt rap anchor
Much of the gear will be in the .75 range on this climb. Excellent moves on great crack climbing. This would be a trade route close to the road. Start in the same corner as *EP2* and head right where the corner splits. Follow excellent lieback moves to a ledge above. Plug some more gear and head to the anchor.
FA: Pat Rinehart, Jason Moncrieff

10 Diggin It 5.7, 5.10b, 5.8+ ☆☆☆☆ 85m

Pitch 1: 5.7, 3 bolts, Gear to 2", 2 bolt rap anchor 36m
Start low on the bulge and go to a big ledge. Move right along the grass to an anchor below the face.
Pitch 2: 5.10b, Gear to 2", 2 bolt rap anchor 30m
The money pitch. Move up right to where you can climb left on to the slab. Bring lots of small to medium gear including plenty of stoppers. Follow thin seams with a crux in the middle. You can move right at the end and chimney to the anchor or climb another thin seam left up the block.
Pitch 3: 5.8+, 1 bolt, Gear to 2", 2 bolt rap anchor 18m
Go direct to the bolt then follow the seam. When you think you want to escape left, hook right through a thin crux mini-roof on small gear. While the occasional large gear may help, TCU's or wires will be best.
Rap the route with a single 60m. Go straight down from the first pitch anchor through the gully.
FA: Jason Moncrieff, Pat Rinehart

11 Shelter in Place 5.9, 5.6 ☆☆☆½ 42m

Pitch 1: 5.9, Gear to 3", 2 bolt rap anchor ☆☆☆ 30m
A unique climb that heads toward the cave feature and starts from the first pitch anchor of *Diggin It*. Move left from the anchor on a wide crack feature that will clean up over time. Move through blocks in the corner until the final airy move into the cave. Belay from under the large roof.
Pitch 2: 5.6, Gear to 3", 2 bolt rap anchor ☆☆☆ 12m
While this pitch isn't especially difficult, it is such a unique and enjoyable climb for Hatcher that it is worth it. Follow the ledge around the corner and get a good dose of exposure before meeting with the anchor for pitch 2 of *Diggin It*. You can do the third pitch of *Diggin It* here to continue the fun or rappel back to the ground with a single 60m, rappel *Diggin It*.
FA: Pat Rinehart, Jason Moncrieff

The Mine Crag 45min

Approach:

The approach to the Mine Crag can be interesting due to the criss-cross of private roads that lead to the crag. The best path to access the Mine Crag is to follow the walkway until the water tunnel entrance. There should be a gap in the railing that leads to a dirt path and a sign that says Mill Loop Trail. Follow this trail staying on the right side of the river and just continue up the valley past all the great boulders. The rail comes and goes but the most legitimate path is to stay off the roads and away from any mining camps while heading directly toward the wall. As of the writing of this book, the Gold Cord Mine, which is located along the dirt road, allowed visitors to the area and nobody seemed to mind us walking along the road. If the traffic was to continue, however, there could be an access issue so it is best to stay in the valley and off the mining road if possible. This cliff is located at the back of the valley beyond all the huts and mines.

Area:

This area saw a lot of development up until 2007, and then it lay quietly waiting for some exposure. Most of the routes have seen little traffic and will clean up over time. It is an interesting area, especially in route finding, as many of the routes have traverses, moss scrambles, or odd starts. There is an upper tier and a lower tier that are tied together with long easy pitches or scrambles around the cliff. From the top of the cliff, a walkoff/scramble down is possible and will probably be easier than trying to rappel, unless you are at an anchor already. Most of the rappels require multiple ropes and even two ropes at 70m wouldn't be a bad idea for the upper pitches. While most of the development in this area was done by Pat Rinehart and Jason Moncrieff, they said there were already a few signs that people had climbed there in years gone past. It's hard to tell what's been climbed, especially at a cliff that can be as confusing as this one. Pay close attention to route lengths and rappel paths as it is easy to get in trouble at this area.

1 No Bolts 5.9+ ☆☆ **60m**

Gear to 2", Gear & Slings anchor

On the far left of the crag, this one move wonder crack is followed by ledges of scrambling up to a large ledge where a big boulder can be used to sling for an anchor. Walkoff unless an anchor has been installed.

FA: Jason Moncrieff, Pat Rinehart

2 Under the Drip 5.10d ☆☆☆☆

6 bolts, Gear to 2", 2 bolt rap anchor

This route starts on the left side of a clean slab. Gear will get you to the first bolt, and one piece may be nice before the next bolt; then it's all sport. Steep face climbing on good holds.

FA: Pat Rinehart, Jason Moncrieff

3 Gold Spot 5.9 ☆☆

Gear to 2", 2 bolt rap anchor

Traverse on to the upper ledge from the right and start at the base of the steep face. Move continuously left along traversing ledges to meet at the same anchor of *Under the Drip.*

FA: Jason Moncrieff, Pat Rinehart

4 PWS Training Run 5.11a ☆☆☆ **35m**

4 bolts, Gear to 2", 2 bolt rap anchor

From the second grass ledge you can start on a flake that takes gear, and then move onto another ledge. You can also walk right along the grass to this higher ledge where a 60m rope may reach from the anchor. Tie knots in the end! Steep climbing through fun blocks with a big reach on the face. Runout from the last bolt on easy ground to the anchor high above the grass.

FA: Pat Rinehart, Jason Moncrieff

5 Paydirt 5.8+ ☆☆☆

5 bolts, Gear to 1", 2 bolt rap anchor

One steep move on big holds lead to a long left traverse on the ledge. It's an easy walk but would definitely lead to painful fall. The next bolt is just over the lip at the end of the ledge. Follow the bolts up and right and then gear to the anchor.

FA: Pat Rinehart, Jason Moncrieff

This wall doesn't get much traffic, but it has a few great lines and most parties will find plenty to climb.

6 Up And At'em 5.10d ☆☆☆
3 bolts, Gear to 1", 2 bolt rap anchor
Start on the first move of *Paydirt* and traverse the ledge left for 3m then look up. There is a bolt in the corner and another one on the roof that leads through the steep and above. Finish in the right angling crack with gear to the anchor.
FA: Jason Moncrieff, Pat Rinehart

7 Goldrunner 5.10d ☆☆☆☆
5 bolts, Gear to 1", 2 bolt rap anchor
Hard moves off the ground, and it doesn't let up much. Follow on the bolts meandering through the steep onto a big ledge. From the ledge go directly up the face on hard, spaced gear or move left and finish on the same crack as the previous two routes.
FA: Pat Rinehart, Jason Moncrieff

8 Date Climbish 5.9 ☆☆☆ **26m**
4 bolts, Gear to 2", 2 bolt rap anchor
Climb 4 bolts on big rest ledges. After the last bolt, follow direct on gear through small corners and on blocks to a high anchor.
FA: Jason Moncrieff, Pat Rinehart

9 Moss Mantle 5.9, 5.8 ☆☆ **86m**
Pitch 1: 5.9, Gear to 2", 2 bolt rap anchor ☆☆ *26m*
Start 2 meters right of *Date Climbish* and climb a black streaked thin crack on small gear until it meets with *Date Climbish* on a ledge. Follow direct on blocks and small corners to the anchor.
Pitch 2: 5.8, Gear to 3", 2 bolt anchor ☆☆ *60m*
Once above the short white face after the corner you can move left onto more rock and continue at a left angle. You'll end up on a big ledge with a 2 bolt anchor but it could be difficult to find.
If you can find the 2 bolt anchor you can lower with two ropes via a 60m rappel with nothing to spare back to the first pitch anchor. If you can't find the bolted anchor, then your best option is to walkoff from the top of the formation by first climbing out.
Pitch 2 Var.1 : 5.8, Gear to 3", Gear anchor ☆☆ *70m*
An adventure pitch, and not all adventures are fun. From the anchor climb into an obvious short corner that is probably wet. From the top move right along ledges below the short face above and into moss ledges and short faces. This pitch is long, and if you go at all off course you'll probably end up simulclimbing even with a 70m rope. At the top of the formation there are cracks to build anchors. It would be better to build an anchor somewhere in the middle.
FA: Jason Moncrieff, Pat Rinehart

10 Razor Arete 5.7 ☆☆☆
Toprope, 2 bolt rap anchor
Another climb up the short block that meets together with the others. Start 3 meters right of *Moss Mantle* and climb the arete. Use gear for directionals above as a swing could put you on to another route.

11 Dry Crack 5.6 ☆☆
Gear to 2", 2 bolt rap anchor
Follows a few thin cracks in the back of the corner. Move left on a slab to meet with *Moss Mantle* at the big ledge. Continue on *Moss Mantle* to the anchor.

12 No Name 5.9 ☆☆
3 bolts, Gear to 1", 2 bolt rap anchor
A slightly overhanging corner for 3 bolts. Once above move left onto the upper face and follow a series of cracks veering right.
FA: Jason Moncrieff, Pat Rinehart

13 By Others 5.8 ☆☆☆
Gear to 1", 2 bolt rap anchor
Follows a crack system up the center of the wall using gear. The climb was probably one of the first put up on the wall. It is a great climb that will improve over time if it gets cleaner.

14 Stellar Cruise 5.10b ☆☆☆☆
Gear to 1", 2 bolt rap anchor
Starts in the center of the wall and moves right on bolts through an excellent slab. Gear between the second and third bolt behind less than trusty flakes.
FA: Pat Rinehart, Jason Moncrieff

15 Claim Jumper 5.6, 5.9 ☆☆☆ **70m**
This climb starts from the anchor of *Paydirt*.
Pitch 1: 5.6, Gear to 2", Gear anchor
This pitch leaves from the anchor of *Paydirt* and goes to the left toward a heavily featured slab. Plenty of runout easy climbing/scrambling as you work your way left on the upper grass ledge. Mostly small gear. Pick a good spot to belay when you find gear along the ledge. This is a long pitch that should get you close to the corner where the second pitch starts.
Pitch 2: 5.9, 3 bolts, Gear to 2", 2 bolt anchor
From the gear anchor, move the rest of the way left across the grass ledge until under a few small roofs. Some small gear and good holds will get you to the first bolt. Enjoyable climbing leads you past the right side of the roof to end on a grassy ledge with the anchor off to the far left.
FA: Pat Rinehart, Jason Moncrieff

The upper area of the crag has a few routes that don't start until the anchor of another climb. You'll have to either climb one of the routes from the ground or scramble into the ones that allow it. These upper routes can often be long with gear belays in the middle or strung together to create extra long pitches. If you plan on doing any of the upper pitches and you don't expect to walkoff, then it is best to bring two ropes and always tie the ends together or tie knots in the end to protect against rappelling off the end of the line.

16 Fin Land 5.4, 5.9 ☆☆☆☆

This climb starts from the anchor of *Moss Mantle.*

Pitch 1: 5.4, Gear to 2", Gear anchor

This is more of an access pitch. From the anchor of *Moss Mantle* climb to the base of the steep face where the route starts and build a gear anchor. This whole route could be done in one pitch with a long rope and bad rope drag.

Pitch 2: 5.9, Gear to 2", 2 bolt rap anchor

This is probably one of the better pitches on the upper wall. Starts on a few blocks that are more loose than desired but heads into some great features of chickenheads with decent protection. End to the left of the giant car sized block above that defies gravity. You can do a full (60m) double rope rappel back to the anchor for *Moss Mantle* or *PWS Training Run* but tie knots in the end. It uses the full rope.

FA: Jason Moncrieff, Pat Rinehart

17 No Fuss, No Gus 5.10a, 5.9 ☆☆☆

Starts from the anchor of *Moss Mantle.*

Pitch 1: 5.10a, Gear to 4", Gear anchor

Climb up grass ledges to a steep face. Some airy and heady moves lead to the crack for a gear anchor.

Pitch 2: 5.9, Gear to 4", 2 bolt anchor

Continue on the crack and traverse left on chickenheads to the crack under a big block where the 4" cam is useful. Traverse left under the next crack into a small corner and go direct from the corner to the giant car sized overhanging block. Move left under the block to end on the same anchor as *Fin Land.* Rappel by using two full 60m or longer ropes back to the anchor for *Moss Mantle.* I've also been told you can rappel back to the anchor for *PWS Training Run* using the full double rope rappel. Tie knots in the ends!

FA: Kelsey Gray, Gus Barber 07.09.2016

18 Lichen This 5.10a ☆☆☆

3 bolts, Gear to 2", 2 bolt anchor

This climb requires a scramble to the base and is on the left side of the second tier of the cliff at a broken corner under a roof. The bolts are easy to find, except the first which is around the corner to the right. Loose blocks of all sizes and some dirt keep the quality down and with some attention this climb could improve. A full 60m rappel with two ropes will get you back to the ledge, walkoff the left side of the cliff.

FA: Pat Rinehart, Jason Moncrieff

Renaissance Wall AM 60min

Approach:
The approach to the Renaissance Wall is not as bad as it looks from the upper Independence parking lot. Walk the paved road and follow a portion of the trail toward Gold Cord Lake on the right. You will pass over a small creek and then head left on a faint trail that goes up the valley on the right side of the small stream. Follow on the grass through the boulders and hook onto the hill following the grass slopes as much as possible. You'll get a good view of the wall from here. Head along the grass staying high and toward the wall.

Area:
The Renaissance Wall is not for the faint of heart. The routes require access pitches, and then the more difficult climbs require some serious commitment. Many will also find the main wall intimidating due to its steepness and bright white color rock, which often means it's overhanging. When you finally get to dig into these climbs, you'll find that the intimidation factor was for a reason. While these climbs are technically not overly difficult, they can be demanding on strength and endurance in a way not normally found in Hatcher Pass.

Those who have been to the wall will tell you about the temperatures. While the rest of Hatcher Pass might be enjoying a nice 70 degree day, the Renaissance Wall will probably be hovering closer to the 50's, and with it spending most of the day in the shade, you'll find yourself colder than expected. It is best to bring a warm jacket here even in the summertime, and the seasons for Renaissance Wall are often different than the surrounding areas, unless you don't mind cold fingers.

1 Warm Up With A Little Fisting 5.10a ☆☆☆ **11m**

Gear to 4", 2 bolt anchor

This short crack climbs the right side of a small tower. Climb the right angling fist crack and end on the top of the formation.

FA: Ben Chriswell, Skine Boynton

2 Tavern Time 5.4, 5.8 ☆☆☆ **66m**

Pitch 1: 5.4, Gear to 2", 2 bolt rap anchor *45m*

This isn't so much a pitch as access to the base of the first two climbs, but it can be nice to be roped and have protection as a few moves are required. Follow the high grass ramp left past a 2 bolt anchor and continue left around the corner on a big block to another anchor below two climbs. This scramble pitch is about 45m and is also the descent path.

Pitch 2: 5.8, 4 bolts, Gear to 2", 2 bolt rap anchor *21m*

From the anchor, move down and left to start on a thin crack. Bolts lead across the enjoyable face and back to gear for the finish. The anchor is high and slightly left after the small corner and can be hard to find. To get back to the ground down scramble the first pitch which is more awkward going down than going up.

FA: Ben Chriswell, Chris Williams

3 SoCal DJ 5.10d ☆☆☆☆☆ **21m**

12 bolts, 2 bolt rap anchor

Climb the first approach pitch for *Tavern Time*. From the belay anchor move right toward a bolt and then follow great features on white rock with some exciting crux moves. Great climb in a great location.

FA: Ben Chriswell, Chris Williams

4 Science is Sorcery 5.11a ☆☆☆ **24m**

7 bolts, Gear to 4", 2 bolt rap anchor

This route starts at a 2 bolt anchor that often has a rope attached that leads around the corner. A somewhat tricky route to follow that will improve as it cleans up. Start on a first crack and then climb through multiple roofs and corners, keeping an eye on the bolts to direct you where to go. From the upper corner look right for a bolt; the anchor is directly above.

FA: Ben Chriswell, Chris Williams

5 L.A.R.Ping On Acid 5.11b/c ☆☆☆☆☆ **24m**

8 bolts, Gear to 1", 2 bolt rap anchor

Scramble the left leaning grass ledge to build a gear anchor before the first bolted anchor on the ledge. The bolted anchor is for a project below. This is also the access ledge for *SoCal DJ* and *Tavern Time* but you stop halfway for this climb. The gear anchor takes BD#2 and #1. From the anchor move right to a corner with gear to the first bolt under a dark patina face. Follow bolts on amazing rock up to the last bolt. A few pieces of gear to .75" will protect the last move to the anchor. Save some strength for the last move.

FA: Ben Chriswell, Erik Pallister, Chris Williams

During the late season it can be really tempting to head to the Renaissance Wall. The temperatures drop significantly as you approach the face, and may scare away most parties.

6 Retroed Art 5.5, 5.11b ☆☆☆☆ 35m

Pitch 1: 5.5, Gear to 2", 2 bolt rap anchor

Follow the left leaning grass scramble ledge till you are under *L.A.R.Ping...* If you continue left to a bolted anchor then you have gone too far. Place a BD#2 and move right passing the start of *L.A.R.Ping...* and continue the scramble to a bolted anchor.

Pitch 2: 5.11b, 3 bolts, Gear to 2", 2 bolt rap anchor

From the anchor follow a corner to the first bolt. This committing climb is heads up climbing that just doesn't seem to let up. Follow the cracks and bolts at a left angle to a hidden anchor you'll be glad to see. From the top of this pitch you can rappel with a 70m rope and just barely reach the lower ledges at the top of the scramble gully. Tie knots in the end! It is best to climb this with a 70m. (35m to ground from anchor)

FA: Ben Chriswell, Erik Pallister, Brady Deal

7 Renaissance Man 5.11c ☆☆☆ 30m

9 bolts, Gear to 3", 2 bolt anchor

This climb leaves from the top of the first pitch of *Retroed Art*. Move right along the ledge into a small bolted corner system. Bolts will lead you to a high crack. Best to do with a 70m rope.

FA: Ben Chriswell, Aaron Thrasher, Chris Williams, Brady Deal, Zach Shlosar, Andy Hoyt

8 Cold Day at the Fair 5.11- ☆☆☆ 24m

10 bolts, Gear to 2", 2 bolt rap anchor

Climb *Scofflaw Rock Jocks* then traverse to a 2 bolt belay anchor. Follow bolts on the slab then head toward the corner. Use gear on horizontals through the steep then follow bolts to the anchor on the ledge.

FA: Ben Chriswell, Noah Burke

9 Walkman & Buttonheads 5.11a ☆☆☆☆☆ 25m

1 bolt, Gear to 3", 2 bolt anchor

This climb can be accessed by first climbing *Scofflaw Rock Jocks* or by scrambling/climbing around the right side to the belay anchor. From the belay, climb toward a splitter crack that splits a few roof systems.

10 The Jester 5.11+ ☆☆☆☆ 21m

7 bolts, Gear to 3", 2 bolt rap anchor

Follow a large ramp at the start then move left to pull over the roof with a bolt. Traverse the seam using gear then follow more bolts direct to the anchor.

FA: Brady Deal, Ben Chriswell

11 Scofflaw Rock Jocks 5.7 ☆☆ 20m

5 bolts, Gear to 3", 2 bolt anchor

An access route for *Walkman & Buttonheads*. From the top of the approach gully, climb a fin of rock on the right hand side. From the top of the fin, move left to a 2 bolt belay anchor for *Walkman & Buttonheads*.

FA: Andy Hoyt

Moai Wall PM 40min

Approach:
Due to the fact that most of the approach is on a well-worn trail to Gold Cord Lake, anyone wanting to get to the crag quickly could easily get there in 20 minutes. Follow the signs to Gold Cord Lake and stay on the well-worn trail. When you reach the lake, look up right and you should see the cliff. Follow around the lake to the right and then head up the grass gully toward the cliff. Do not go around the lake, but instead head up the hillside.

Area:
This small but enjoyable area has an excellent view of the lake and one of the better slab climbs around. This is a great place to bring beginners because you can climb all of the routes from one anchor; but be careful about scrambling around, as there is plenty of loose rock in the gully.

1 Easy Angle 5.5r ☆☆ **28m**
Gear to 2", 2 bolt rap anchor
From the low point on the slab follow a grassy corner up easy climbing to a crack that diagonals toward the anchor. Dirty and easy if runout.
FA: Chris Williams, Lang Van Dommelen 2015

2 Birdman Cult 5.9 ☆☆☆ **27m**
3 bolts, Gear to 1", 2 bolt rap anchor
Follow a short crack halfway up the cliff with somewhat awkward gear to 2 high bolts on green rock. Continue on the face to the anchor.
FA: Chris Williams, Lang Van Dommelen 2015

3 Rapa Nui 5.10a ☆☆☆☆☆ **26m**
7 bolts, 2 bolt rap anchor
Follow a thin seam to the first bolt and then put on your friction shoes for some great slab moves through thin features.
FA: Lang Van Dommelen, Chris Williams, Dan Linnell 2015

4 Two Canoes 5.6 ☆☆ **23m**
Gear to 2", 2 bolt rap anchor
This climbs a thin crack with occasionally flaring gear. Walk the ledge left to the anchor.
FA: Dan Linnell, Lang Van Dommelen, Chris Williams 2015

5 Easter Island 5.7 ☆☆☆ **22m**
Gear to .75", 2 bolt rap anchor
This is a fun climb when dry and still decent when wet. Follow the left angling crack in the back of the corner all the way to the anchor.
FA: Chris Williams, Lang Van Dommelen 2015

Glossary

Abseil - The process by which a climber may descend on a fixed rope. Also known as Rappel for anyone who can't pronounce or spell this word.
Aid climbing - A form of rock climbing that requires artificial assistance, i.e. ropes, and other protection to ascend.
Anchor - A fail-safe (often as safe as you make it) attachment point for protection.
Approach - The path or route to the start of a technical climb. Can be extremely hazardous or in the case of Hatcher Pass, a very long, wet slog.
Arete - The outside corner of rock.
Ascender - A device for ascending on a rope. A mechanical ascender is called a jumar and the process of ascending the rope is often called jugging.
ATC - A proprietary type of belay device, ATC stands for Air Traffic Controller.
Back-clipping - A hazardous mistake that can be made while lead climbing. The belay rope is clipped into a quickdraw in the wrong direction causing an increase in friction on the rope and an increase in the likelihood of the rope becoming unclipped during a fall.
Bail - To give up on a climb, go home, have a snack, and watch the news.
Belay - Protecting a climber from falling using a rope.
Belay device - A mechanical device used when belaying. Many types of belay devices exist, including ATC, GriGri, Reverso, Sticht plate, eight, tuber, and the Munter hitch. Some belay devices may also be used as descenders.
Beta - Advice and/or instructions on how to successfully complete a particular climbing route.
Bolt - An anchor-point permanently drilled into the rock and made of metal.
Bomb-proof anchor - A totally secure anchor, or set of anchors. Also known as a bomber.
Bouldering - The practise of climbing on large boulders. Typically this is close to the ground, so protection takes the form of crash pads and spotting instead of belay ropes.
Bucket - A huge hand hold often called a Jug or "Thank God" hold.
Buildering - The art of climbing on buildings. Note that this is often illegal.
Cam - To affix using counter-pressure. A spring-loaded device used to place protection.
Carabiner - Metal rings with spring-loaded gates, used as connectors. Also known as a biner.
Chalk - A compound used to improve grip by absorbing sweat. It is actually gymnastics chalk, usually magnesium carbonate. Its use is controversial in some areas.
Chalk bag - A hand-sized holder for a climber's chalk that is usually clipped or tied onto the climber's harness for easy access during a climb.
Chock - A mechanical device, or a wedge, used to attach anchors into cracks. A chockstone is a rock wedged somewhere that can used as an anchor or hold.
Clean - To remove equipment from a route. A route that is free of loose vegetation and rocks. To complete a climb without falling or resting on the rope. Also see Redpoint.
Climbing area - A region that has numerous climbing routes.
Climbing command - A short phrase used for communication between a climber and a belayer. Such as, "Promise you'll eat my body!!!!" as you fall past your belayer.
Climbing gym - Specialized indoor climbing centers.
Climbing shoe - Footwear designed specifically for climbing. Usually well fitting, with a rubber sole.
Climbing technique - Particular techniques, or moves, commonly applied in climbing.
Clipping in - The process of attaching to belay lines or anchors for protection.
Crack climbing - To ascend on a rock face by wedging body parts into cracks, i.e. not face climbing. See Jamming.
Crag - An area with climbing routes.
Crank - To pull on a hold as hard as possible.
Crash pad - A thick mat used to soften landings or to cover hazardous objects in the event of a fall. Buy an expensive one or grab a mattress.

Crimp - A small but positive hold. The process of holding onto a crimp.
Crux - The most difficult portion of a climb.
Daisy chain - A type of sling with multiple sewn or tied loops. In many situations this can be more versatile than a normal sling.
Dead hang - To hang limp, such that weight is held by arm tension rather than muscles.
Deadman - A dynamic climbing technique in which the hold is grabbed at the apex of upward motion. This technique places minimal strain on both the hold and the arms.
Deadpoint - The apex of an upward dynamic move.
Deck - The ground. To hit the ground, usually the outcome of a fall. Try avoiding this.
Descender - A device for controlled descent on a rope. Many belay devices may be used as descenders, including ATCs, eights, or even carabiners. Gravity alone is not a proper descender.
Dialed - To have complete understanding of a particular climbing move or route.
Dihedral - The inside corner of rock.
Downclimb - To descend by climbing downward, typically after completing a climb or after getting stuck and realizing you should never free-solo again.
Dynamic rope - A slightly elastic rope that softens falls to some extent. Also tends to be damaged less severely by heavy loads. Compare with Static rope.
Dyno - A dynamic move to grab a hold that would otherwise be out of reach. Non-climbers might call this a lunge.
Edge - A thin ledge on the rock.
Edging - Using the edge of the climbing shoe on a foothold.
Egyptian - A climbing technique used to reduce tension in arms while holding a side grip.
Eight - A belay device or descender. Named from its appearance as the digit "8".
Exposure - State of openness with relation to the distance of a fall. The reason to scream when looking down.
Face climbing - To ascend on a rock face using finger hold and edges, i.e. not rack climbing.
Fall - Undesirable downward motion. Hopefully stopped by a rope, otherwise seek medical attention and climbing commands for what to say next.
First ascent - The first successful completion of a route.
Fist jam - A type of jam using the hand by jamming it into a crack.
Fixed rope - A rope that has a fixed attachment point. Commonly used for abseiling or aid climbing, all are skeptical and should not be fully trusted.
Flake - A thin slab of rock detached from the main face.
Flapper - An injury consisting of a piece of loose (flapping) skin. A climber will usually just repair these with sticky tape.
Flash - To successfully and cleanly complete a climbing route on the first attempt.
Follow - What the second, or belayer, does after the climber has finished.
Free climbing - Climbing without unnatural aids, other than used for protection.
Grade - Intended as an objective measure of the technical difficultly of a particular climbing route or bouldering problem. More often is highly subjective, however.
GriGri - A belay device designed to be easy to use and safe for beginners because it is self-locking under load. Invented and manufactured by Petzl.
Gripped - Scared, over gripping to the point of failure.
Hand Traverse - Traversing without any footholds.
Hangdog - While lead climbing, to hang on the rope or an anchor for a rest.
Hanging Belay - Belaying at a point such that the belayer is suspended.
Harness - Climbing equipment used for attaching a rope to a person.
Haul bag - A large and often unwieldy bag into which supplies and climbing equipment may be thrown.
Headwall - The region of a cliff or rock face that steepens dramatically.
Helmet - Also known as a brain bucket. It can save your life, but only while worn. Mandatory Alaskan piece of climbing equipment.
Hexcentric - A protective device. It is a hexagonal nut attached to a wire loop. The nut is inserted into a crack and it holds through counter-pressure. Often just termed Hex.

Honed - To be in peak mental and physical fitness for climbing. The sharp end of a #2 pencil.
Hook - Equipment used in aid climbing. A climbing technique.
Jamming - Wedging a body part into a crack. See also Bob Marley.
Jug hold - A large hold, also known just as a jug or bucket.
Klemheist knot - An alternative to the prusik knot, useful when the climber is short of cord but has plenty of webbing.
Knots - Climbers rely on many different knots for anchoring oneself to a mountain, joining two ropes together, slings for climbing up the rope, etc.
Lead climbing - A form of climbing in which the climber places anchors and attaches the belay rope as they climb.
Lieback - Or layback. A climbing move that involves pulling with the hands while pushing on the feet.
Locking carabiner - A carabiner with a locking gate, to prevent accidental release of the rope.
Mantle - A move used to surmount a ledge or feature in the rock in the absence of any useful holds directly above.
Match - To use one hold for two limbs, or to swap limbs on a particular hold.
Mountain rescue - A friendly team of people that will come and rescue you after an injury or accident.
Move - Application of a specific climbing technique to progress on a climb.
Multi-pitch climbing - Climbing on routes that are too long for a single belay rope.
Munter hitch - A simple hitch that is often used for belaying without a mechanical belay device. Otherwise known as an Italian hitch or a Friction hitch.
Nut - A metal wedge attached to a wire loop that is inserted into cracks for protection. Also called a Stopper in this guide.
Off-width - A crack that is too wide for effective hand or foot jams. It is as pleasant as it sounds.
Onsight - A clean ascent, with no prior practice or beta.
Open book - An inside angle in the rock.
Overhang - A section of rock or ice that is angled beyond vertical. See Roof.
Pinkpoint - To complete a lead climb without falling or resting on the rope (hang dogging), but with pre-placed protection and carabiners. Also see Clean and Redpoint.
Pitch - The portion of a climb between two belay points.
Piton - A metal spike that may be hammered into ice or flaws in rock.
Protection - Process of setting equipment or anchors for safety. Equipment or anchors used for preventing falls. Commonly known as "pro".
Prusik - A knot used for ascending a rope. To use a prusik knot for ascending a rope.
Quickdraw - Used to attach a freely running rope to anchors or chocks. Sometimes called quickies and done in parking garages.
Rack - The set of equipment carried up a climb.
Rappel - The process by which a climber may descend on a fixed rope. Also known as Abseil.
Redpoint - To complete a lead climb without falling or resting on the rope (hang dogging). Also see Clean and Pinkpoint.
Roof - Horizontal overhang. See Overhang.
Rope - An essential item of climbing equipment.
Route - The path of a particular climb, or a predefined set of moves.
Runner - Another term for Sling.
Runout - The span between two points of protection. A long portion of a route without adequate protection.
Scrambling - Non-technical climbing.
Scree - Loose, broken rock that climbers can never seem to avoid.
Second - A climber who follows the lead, or first, climber.
Sharp end - The end of the belay rope that is attached to the lead climber.
Side grip - Use of a horizontal hold.
Sit start - Starting a climb from a position in which the climber is sitting on the floor. Often confusing to those who stay mostly on the rope.
Slab - A relatively flat and featureless block of rock.

Sling - Webbing sewn, or tied, into a loop.
Smearing - To use friction on the sole of the climbing shoe, in the absence of any useful footholds.
Solo climbing - Climbing without any protection.
Sport climbing - Sport climbing routes tend to be well protected with pre-placed bolt-anchors.
Spotting - An alternative to belaying commonly used during bouldering. A friend of the climber stands beneath them and prevents awkward falls or falls onto hazards.
Static rope - A non-elastic rope. Compare with Dynamic rope.
Stem - The simultaneous use of two widely spaced footholds.
Stopper - A wedge-shaped nut. A knot used to prevent the rope running through a piece of equipment.
Top rope - To belay from a fixed anchor point above the climb.
Traverse - To climb in a horizontal direction. A feature of a rock that can allow progress in a horizontal direction.
Undercling - A hold or flake that is upside down.
V-grade - A technical grading system for bouldering problems, invented by John Sherman.
Webbing - Hollow and flat rope, mainly used to make runners and slings.
Weighting - Resting by hanging on the belay rope.
Wired - To have the moves required for completing a climb memorized.
Yosemite Decimal System - A numerical system for rating the difficulty of walks, hikes, and climbs in the United States of America. The rock climbing (5.x) portion of the scale is the most common climb grading system used in the USA.
Zipper fall - A fall in which each piece of protection fails in turn.

The Mile High Wall, a crag for future editions...

Accommodations

If you've made your way to Alaska, then you're going to need a place to stay. This area is primarily for those who are looking for accommodations that don't include some Alaska climber bum's basement.

There is camping in many areas of Hatcher Pass, such as at the end of Archangel Road. However, there are also accommodations near the park that are excellent for a night's stay. As of 2016 the park officials have started to enforce some frustrating rules for climbers. If you are anywhere between the Reed Lakes parking area or the paved road you cannot camp near the road and must be at least 0.5mi away before dropping your tent. There are also fee stations for parking, which is sort of ridiculous considering the quality of the road to Archangel. In 2020, due to the death of "Hap" Wurlitzer, the Hatcher Pass Lodge closed. This was the closest you could be to the crags and still sleep inside a building.

Government Peak Picnic Site **$**

Parking is $5. Located at Mile 11 on Hatcher Pass Road. There are camping possibilities nearby. Picnic tables are also at the site.
http://dnr.alaska.gov/parks/aspunits/matsu/govpeakcamp.htm
☎ 907.269.8400

Hatcher Pass B&B **$$$**

They have a few beautiful cabins for rent. The average cost is $100 per night. Summer rates are usually higher.
9000 N. Palmer Fishhook Road, Palmer, AK 99645
http://www.hatcherpassbb.com/
☎ 907.745.6788 or 1.877.745.6788

Alaska Garden Gate B&B **$$$**

Located around 12 miles from Hatcher Pass. Expect to pay $89 or more depending on the room. They have rooms as well as cottages with full kitchens. Costs will rise during the busy season but they do have discounts for each additional person in your party.
950 S. Trunk Road, Palmer, AK 99645
http://www.gardengatebnb.com/
☎ 907.746.2333

Jack Rambac inspecting the lodgings of past miners on the trail to Gold Chord Lake. This beautiful and easy hike ends at the crystal clear waters of Gold Chord Lake. Moai Wall is just a short hike from there is worth a good afternoon.

Alaska Birch Cottages **$$$**

For the climbers who don't mind spending a little extra. Beautiful cottages in a great setting but expect to spend at least $200 per night. They are located in Wasilla.
http://alaskabirchcottages.com/
☎ 907.745.0558pads, accessible picnic tables, and fire grills.
13 miles from downtown Juneau on Mendenhall Lake.
Open May 15 - September 15
Some reservations can be made at:
www.ReserveUSA.com

Kayla Rowe rappelling after climbing Toto with her father, Jay Rowe. (Courtesy Jay Rowe)

YDS	UIAA	FR	AUS	SAX	CIS	SCA	BRA	UK	
5.2	II	1	10	II	III	3			D
5.3	III	2	11	III	III+	3+			
5.4	IV-	3	12		IV-	4			VD
5.5	IV IV+		13		IV	4+			S
5.6	V-	4	14		IV+	5-		4a	HS
5.7	V		15	VIIa		5		4b	VS
5.8	V+	5a	16	VIIb	V-	5+	4/4+	4c	HVS
5.9	VI-	5b	17	VIIc		6-	5/5+	5a	E1
5.10a	VI	5c	18	VIIIa	V	6	6a		
5.10b	VI+	6a		VIIIb			6b	5b	E2
5.10c	VII-	6a+	19			6+			
5.10d	VII	6b	20	VIIIc	V+		6c		E3
5.11a	VII+	6b+		IXa		7-	7a	5c	
5.11b		6c	21	IXb		7			
5.11c	VIII-	6c+	22		VI-	7+	7b		E4
5.11d	VIII	7a	23	IXc			7c	6a	
5.12a		7a+	24			8-	8a		E5
5.12b	VIII+	7b	25	Xa	VI	8	8b		
5.12c	IX-	7b+	26	Xb			8c		
5.12d	IX	7c	27			8+	9a	6b	E6
5.13a		7c+	28	Xc		9-	9b		
5.13b	IX+	8a	29				9c		
5.13c	X-	8a+	30			9	10a	6c	E7
5.13d	X	8b	31	XIa	VI+		10b		
5.14a		8b+	32				10c	7a	E8
5.14b	X+	8c	33	XIb		9+			
5.14c	XI-	8c+		XIc				7b	E9
5.14d	XI	9a							

Climbing Guides and Books

Alaska Rock Climbing Guide
4th edition (2021)
Kelsey Gray

Dghelaya: A Hatcher Pass Climbing Guide
1st edition (2021)
Kelsey Gray

Alaska Ice Guide
1st edition (2019)
Kelsey Gray, Burrell Nickeson,
Chris Lindsey

Koh Tao Rock Climbing (Thailand)
Rakkup App Guide
1st edition (2019)
Kelsey Gray

Just Us Down Here
Poems
1st edition (2018)
Kelsey Gray & Rena McDonell

Alaska Rock Climbing Guide
3rd edition (2017)
Kelsey Gray

climbak.com

It's been wonderful being able to write the rock and ice climbing guides for Alaska. I have worked with some amazing co-authors, artists, and designers. I hope you enjoy these books as much as I enjoyed making them.

Found Wandering : Poems for the lost
1st edition (2016)
Kelsey Gray

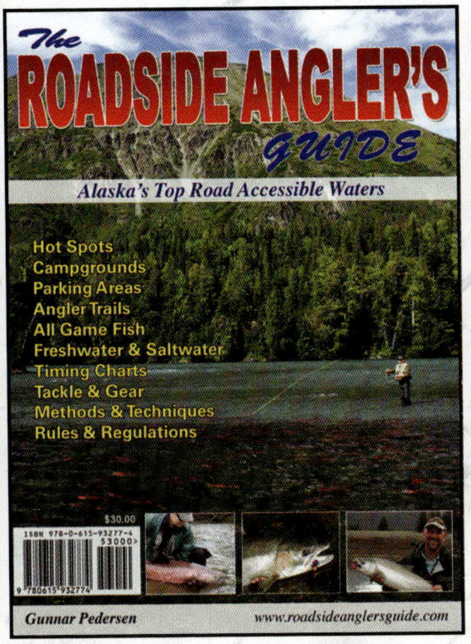

The Roadside Angler's Guide
1st edition (2016)
Gunnar Pedersen (author)
Kelsey Gray (publishing & design)

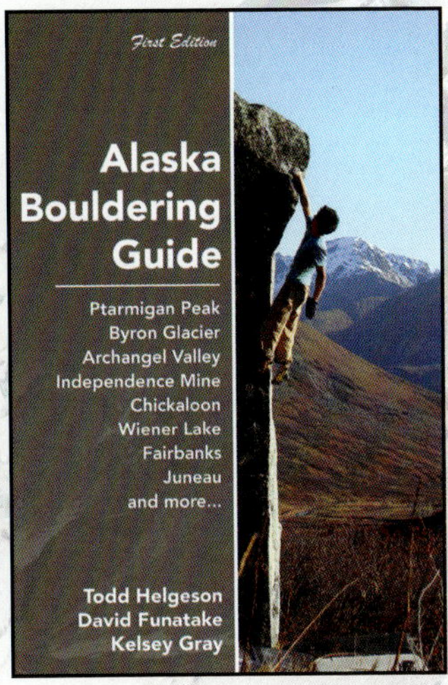

Alaska Bouldering Guide
1st edition (2013)
Todd Helgeson, David Funatake,
Kelsey Gray

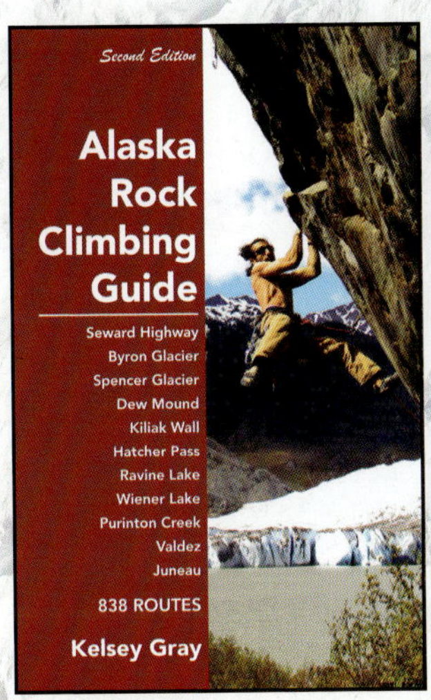

Alaska Rock Climbing Guide
2nd edition (2012)
Kelsey Gray

Alaska Rock Climbing Guide
1st edition (2009)
Kelsey Gray

Freedom of the Soul: Words and Writings
of a Confused Wanderer
1st edition (2006)
Kelsey Gray

climbak.com

Index

Emergency Contact

Let's face it, if you climb long enough you'll probably need to call emergency services. It's not something to look forward to but just in case I've included this section. These emergency services will hopefully help you discover the best way to get assistance. Often when climbing in Alaska you'll find you get no phone service at all. The general suggestion in that case is to go in the last direction you knew you had a good signal. It can sometimes be easier to send a text than call. Either way it is suggested that you bring a cell phone or other contact device. So good luck out there, wear your helmet, file a trip report and try not to use this section if you can help it.

There are many places in Hatcher Pass where cell phones do not work, especially in areas of Archangel Valley. If you do have an emergency, drive toward town. Usually within 1 or 2 miles reception will return. If you do not have a cell phone there are emergency phones located at:

Hatcher Pass Lodge - Mile 17

Hatcher Pass Lodge is unfortunately closed until further notice do the passing of "Hap" Wurlitzer. We hope they will be able to reopen again in the future.

911

The first number to call; Palmer dispatch for Alaska State Troopers.

☎ 911

Alaska State Troopers

Is the same as calling 911 or is a good number for non life threatening emergencies.

☎ 907.745.2131

State Park Rangers

For questions pertaining to the park or a backup emergency number.

☎ 907.745.3975 or 907.745.2827